POINTS OF VIEW

POINTS OF VIEW

Stories of Psychopathology

James E. Mitchell, M.D.

BRUNNER-ROUTLEDGE
ALERE FLAMMAM
Taylor & Francis Group

USA	Publishing Office:	BRUNNER-ROUTLEDGE
		A member of the Taylor & Francis Group
		325 Chestnut Street
		Philadelphia, PA 19106
		Tel: (215) 625-8900
		Fax: (215) 625-2940
	Distribution Center:	BRUNNER-ROUTLEDGE
		A member of the Taylor & Francis Group
		7625 Empire Drive
		Florence, KY 41042
		Tel: 1-800-634-7064
		Fax: 1-800-248-4724
UK		BRUNNER-ROUTLEDGE
		A member of the Taylor & Francis Group
		27 Church Road
		Hove
		E. Sussex, BN3 2FA
		Tel.: +44 (0) 1273 207411
		Fax: +44 (0) 1273 205612

POINTS OF VIEW: Stories of Psychopathology

1 2 3 4 5 6 7 8 9 0

Printed by George H. Buchanan Co., Philadelphia, PA, 2001.
Cover design by Rob Williams.

A CIP catalog record for this book is available from the British Library.
    The paper in this publication meets the requirements of the ANSI Standard Z39.48-1984 (Permanence of Paper).

Library of Congress Cataloging-in-Publication Data

Mitchell, James E. (James Edward), 1947-
    Points of view : stories of psychology / James E. Mitchell.
        p. cm.

    1. Psychology, Pathological—Case studies.   I. Title.
    RC465.M56 2000
    616.89—dc21   00-041355

ISBN 1-58391-005-0 (alk. paper)

To my wonderful children,
James and Katherine

CONTENTS

PART VI
SOMATOFORM DISORDERS

PART VII
FACTITIOUS DISORDER

PART XI
PERSONALITY DISORDERS

ACKNOWLEDGMENTS

Before proceeding, there are a few individuals I would like to thank. First, my thanks to Bernadette Capelle, Acquisitions Editor at Brunner-Routledge, who was open to my ideas, kindly agreed to publish this book, and with whom it was a pleasure to work. Second, I would like to thank my best friend and wife, Karen—certainly for her patience with my long work hours and frequent travel. For her help with this book, though, a special thanks. The book was her idea, and many of the scenarios were generated by us as a team, often concocted when we were driving somewhere. If readers find some of the stories particularly interesting, those are undoubtedly the ones she influenced most heavily. I would also like to thank Ron Erickson, the administrator at the Research Institute where I conduct my research. Ron is always supportive of my projects and goes out of his way to make sure I have the necessary staff to carry them out. Last, I would like to thank my secretary Cathy Lefebvre who typed this book. She is highly talented, very hard working, and resourceful. Having Cathy as my secretary in the last few years has simplified my life enormously.

PREFACE

This book is designed to provide students at various levels of experience and training with examples illustrating the problems of individuals with various forms of psychopathology. The work is designed primarily for students who are studying descriptive psychopathology, including psychiatric residents, medical students on psychiatry rotations, graduate students in psychology, or students in various related mental health fields including psychiatric nursing, social work, and school counseling.

The stories are written to illustrate the key elements of psychopathology for these various disorders. They are written from two perspectives: the perspective of the individual who has the disorder, and the perspective of someone else in their environment (e.g., a family member, friend, doctor). The thoughts of these individuals are given in parentheses. This design was chosen as a means to attempt to illustrate not only how people with these disorders think and feel themselves but also how they appear to the people around them. The emphasis, therefore, is on the difficulties, often the suffering, experienced by people with various mental illnesses, and also on the adverse impact these illnesses have on others, which is usually substantial. The stories are written in a style I hope readers will find accessible and interesting. All the people in these stories are my invention. None are based on patients I have evaluated or treated.

Altogether, 24 disorders are illustrated, broken down into 11 categories. The organization is based on the *Diagnostic and Statistical Manual of Mental Disorders*, Fourth Edition (DSM-IV), of the American Psychiatric Association (APA, 1994), and much of the material I present is derived from this source. The DSM-IV is the document which presents the nomenclature most widely used worldwide for the diagnosis of psychiatric disorders. As we will see, the DSM-IV uses a categorical system of diagnosis. The development of the DSM system has markedly improved our ability to reliably diagnose our patients and, of most importance, to match patients to the appropriate treatment. However, this work is still in evolution, and no one currently believes that the nomenclature as it currently exists actually is in its final form and "carves nature at its joints." It is a working document—the best we have for now. However, research in the field of neurosciences in general and psychiatry in particular is evolving rapidly, and some of the material in the DSM-IV has already been superceded. Therefore, it is important for readers to see this categorical system as a useful tool to use clinically in working with patients and in communicating with other health professionals, but not to regard it as the final, complete terminology. Likewise we know that mental disorders usually do not exist in simple pure form. Comorbidity, or the presence of two or more conditions, is very common (e.g., most patients with eating disorders also meet criteria for major depressive disorder; most individuals with one anxiety disorder meet criteria for a second). Therefore, although the system seems to paint a straightforward, simple picture with firm boundaries between conditions, clinically the separations are less crisp.

Relative to the organization of the book, this work confines itself to disorders that are usually present in adulthood. I have attempted to choose the particularly common forms of psychopathology (e.g., depression), and some rarer forms of particular interest (e.g., body dysmorphic disorder, trichotillomania). I've organized the sections as they occur in the DSM-IV, beginning with "Delirium, Dementia, and Amnesic and Other Cognitive Disorders" and progressing through "Personality Disorders." Each chapter in each section is devoted to one disorder and is broken down into six subsections:

1) An introduction that introduces the disorder and the stories and provides some questions to be considered when reading the stories.
2) The diagnostic criteria as they appear in the DSM-IV. This information is reprinted with permission.
3) The stories themselves—one from the vantage point of the individual who suffers from the mental disorder, and the other from the standpoint of someone else.
4) A discussion of the stories, with particular attention as to which diagnostic criteria are fulfilled or not fulfilled. Emphasis is also placed on some general information about the disorder, much of it abstracted from the DSM-IV (its prevalence, gender ratio, heritability). Differential diagnosis (what alternative disorders need to be ruled out) is also often discussed. Lastly, treatment is briefly mentioned.
5) Additional questions that might be used as discussion points in a class or seminar.
6) Reference to the DSM-IV and suggested readings that may be of interest to those who would like to approach the subject in greater detail.

In reading these stories, one must remember that the fictional examples offered represent only one "variant" of the disorder illustrated. While the variability in symptoms across diagnostic categories will be obvious, the variability within categories is not illustrated. Most of the disorders we will discuss can present in many different ways; thus, attention to the diagnostic criteria that are not illustrated is also important.

Lastly, I urge the readers of this text to notice not just the illnesses themselves, but the people who have these illnesses. These are people like you and me, who for various reasons (e.g., genetics, life experience) develop a mental illness. They don't ask for these illnesses, nor do they do anything to deserve them. They are victims. The days are long past when any educated person could possibly see mental illness as something people bring on themself, or "deserve" because of what they have done. So, as part of your study of these people, pay attention to your reaction to them and your biases about them, since these variables will color any future work you may do with mentally ill people.

☐ References

American Psychiatric Association. (1994). *Diagnostic and statistical manual of mental disorders* (4th ed.). Washington, DC: Author.

I

DELIRIUM, DEMENTIA, AMNESTIC, AND OTHER COGNITIVE DISORDERS

In this section we will focus on two disorders: delirium and dementia of the Alzheimer's type. Although lay people often confuse the terms delirium and dementia, they describe very different phenomena, as we will see. Of particular importance to this differentiation is reversibility, which is frequent in delirium and does not happen in dementia. In the DSM-IV, another category, amnestic disorders, characterized by an isolated disorder of memory, is included as well.

In considering the two disorders we will discuss in this section, notice that these are very severe forms of psychopathology. Those affected are—or in the case of dementia, become—globally dysfunctional. Because of this, delirium often occurs during or results in hospitalization, and dementia often results in the need for ongoing supervision and care.

CHAPTER 1

Delirium

☐ Introduction

The pivotal symptoms of delirium are a disturbance of consciousness (how fully aware one is of one's surroundings) coupled with a change in cognitive functioning of thinking, that are not accounted for by some other condition. Delirium usually develops fairly rapidly over a period of hours to days, and runs a highly variable and often fluctuating course. If the cause of the delirium can be ascertained and corrected (e.g., an underlying infection, a disturbance of serum electrolytes), the disorder may resolve fairly rapidly. In the DSM-IV system, delirium is classified as being due to a medical condition, being substance induced, due to multiple etiologies (unfortunately often the case), or "not otherwise specified."

In the following stories, please pay particular attention to several points:

1) How quickly did the disturbance develop in this case?
2) What is the nature of the cognitive deficit? Is there evidence of memory impairment? Disorientation? What else is abnormal?
3) What would the likely etiology be for the delirium for this case?

☐ Diagnostic Criteria

(American Psychiatric Association, *Diagnostic and Statistical Manual of Mental Disorders,* 4th Edition)

A. Disturbance of consciousness (i.e., reduced clarity of awareness of the environment) with reduced ability to focus, sustain, or shift attention.
B. A change in cognition (such as memory deficit, disorientation, language disturbance) or the development of a perceptual disturbance that is not better accounted for by a preexisting, established, or evolving dementia.
C. The disturbance develops over a short period of time (usually hours to days) and tends to fluctuate during the course of the day.
D. There is evidence from the history, physical examination, or laboratory findings that the disturbance is caused by the direct physiological consequences of a general medical condition.

☐ The Stories

I

Samantha Wright got off the hospital elevator on the fourth floor and started down the B corridor toward her father's room. Samantha saw this as a routine visit, and was not really concerned about her father's welfare. Her father, Malcolm Jefferies, had undergone hip replacement surgery the day before. However, when she had seen him the previous evening he was awake, in reasonably good spirits, and was already evidencing some of his sense of humor that always made him such a hit with Samantha's children. Samantha's mother, Betty, had spent this afternoon with Malcolm, and had then come over to Samantha's house to sit with the children while Samantha visited her father after dinner. Samantha felt a little uncomfortable visiting a hospital—she always did—she wasn't sure why, but she was sure that this was true of most people. There was something about being around the sick and infirm that upset her.

(Thank goodness he has a private room). She paused briefly to chat with the nurse who was charting outside of Mr. Jefferies' room. The nurse reassured her that things were going fine. His blood pressure had been a bit elevated—Samantha knew he had a history of high blood pressure—but they were giving him medication to bring it under control, and there was nothing to worry about. He had started eating, and was tolerating food quite well. They were pleased with his progress. Dr. Ranson, the orthopedic surgeon, would be by to see him on rounds sometime that evening.

As she turned into the room she was surprised by the number of plants and flowers in vases occupying just about every flat surface in the room. Her father and mother had lots of friends. She called out a cheerful "Hi Dad, it's Sam," while pausing a moment before pushing the curtain back in case he needed privacy. As she looked down at him she was surprised by his somewhat stern, perplexed look. She had expected the usual bright smile and wink, but he seemed at first not to recognize her.

"Hi Dad, it's Sam. How are you feeling? Is everything all right?" (Why is he staring at me. I don't think he recognizes me).

"Oh, hi. Sorry. I was thinking about something else," replied her father slowly, but he still seemed concerned and perplexed, and to some extent almost disinterested in her. His attention seemed to wander from her face to the television (he never watches television), to the flowers, to the window, toward the traffic in the street below. When she touched his arm or said his name he would look back, then his attention would wander off again.

"Dad, are you okay?" Samantha's concern continued to escalate (I wonder if something has gone wrong. He seems ill, confused. I wonder if he has had a stroke?)

His attention then seemed fixed on the sheet covering his chest and abdomen. He kept brushing at it with his hand as if to remove something there—something Samantha couldn't see—and at the time was mumbling something about "bugs."

Samantha pushed the call button for the nurse. She was very concerned. She pressed down on her father's hand. "Dad, what's wrong? Has something happened? Tell me what is going on. Are you hurting somewhere?"

In a fairly clear deliberate voice he slowly replied, "Oh well, I guess it's time for me to go to bed," and attempted to sit up and swing his legs over the side of the bed. Samantha restrained him forcefully, pressing her body down and holding down on his leg (I hope I'm not hurting him) as the nurse came in.

"He's trying to get out of bed. He seems confused," said Samantha. Using the intercom, the nurse called for assistance. She put her face down close to Mr. Jefferies' face, "Malcolm, do you know where you are Malcolm?" He seemed to gaze away from her, and she shook his shoulder as she repeated the question.

He seemed irritated and said back in a somewhat menacing tone,

"Who let you in here?" Another nurse and a nursing student came into the room. The first nurse took charge of the situation, "Malcolm has become confused and is trying to get out of bed. Please go down the hall and get the soft restraints. Sally, you page Dr. Ranson and tell him what has happened. Mrs. Wright, I think you should probably wait in the hall for a few minutes."

Samantha Wright stepped out in the hall, her mind reeling (What could this be? A stroke? Alzheimer's?). She spotted a public phone down the hall and walked toward it, fumbling in her purse for thirty-five cents. Her mother picked up the phone after the second ring.

"Mom, I'm with Dad and something is wrong. I thought you said everything was fine this afternoon when you were here?"

Her mother was shocked. "What's wrong? Everything was fine! What's happened?"

An hour later, after a brief examination, Dr. Ranson met with Mrs. Wright in a small office off the nursing station. He was clearly tired, but patient and concerned. Samantha was again surprised, as she had been when she first met him, by his youthfulness.

"Mrs. Wright, I can reassure you that this is not a stroke, or anything like that. I believe it is probably what we call delirium. Usually it is reversible. It happens not uncommonly to elderly people after surgery. There may be some specific reason, like an infection, or it may relate to your father's blood pressure, which has been a little difficult to control. We are going to run some tests to see if we can find out what is going on. Also, I'm going to ask Dr. Maudsley, a psychiatrist, to see your father. He is an expert in this sort of thing and he will probably recommend some medication which will be helpful for your father. I'll call your mother and apprise her of all of this."

II

Things had gotten quite confusing for Malcolm Jefferies. He wasn't exactly sure what was going on. First, he seemed so tired. He just couldn't keep his eyes open. At other times he felt very anxious, like he was going to crawl out of his skin. He was aware that people would come and go, but it wasn't at all clear why they were keeping him here. Had he done something wrong? Was someone trying to harm him? (And where are they keeping me?) At times he thought he was in his bedroom, and at other times in some other strange place, but what kind of a place? It just didn't make sense, and nobody was telling him anything. He was frightened; perhaps his life was in danger, and he felt this terrible pain in his hip. They had him tied down, and they had put some sort of thing on his hip that was causing him a great deal of pain. (What is it? Bandages? A cast? Some sort of torture device?) He looked for his watch to tell the time, but his watch wasn't on his arm. He just couldn't remember. Was it day or night? Summer or winter?

☐ Discussion

The patient, Malcolm Jefferies, has recently undergone surgery, and the post-surgery recovery phase is a time of great risk for the development of delirium. We have evidence that the problem developed over a period of a few hours since the story indicates that he was evidently fine in the afternoon, but then symptomatic by the time the daughter visits in the evening. Until alerted to the problem by the daughter, the nurses were unaware of the problem as well, again suggesting that it developed quite recently given the fact that patients would be checked quite frequently on a surgery ward (although it is possible that the patient may have been confused for some time and staff had not noticed).

  We have evidence that the patient is disoriented (he is not sure where he is, what time it is, or what has happened to him), clearly he is having memory impairment (he doesn't appear to recall the surgery or recognize his daughter), and appears to be hallucinating (brushing something off the front of his shirt, perhaps "bugs" that he believes he sees, that are not really there). Relative to possible etiologies, Dr. Ranson suggests several in his remarks. He mentions that the elderly are at risk for this problem, particularly after surgery. He also mentions that other possible risk factors in this case might be an infection, and the patient's hypertension which has evidently been difficult to control.

  Delirium can be characterized as evidencing multiple cognitive deficits. These include disorientation, problems with memory, and problems with speech and language. Disturbances of perception, including hallucinations (seeing things that aren't there, hearing voices or sounds that have no origin in the environment) are also quite common and can be very upsetting to the patient. This disorder usually begins over a short period of time and often runs a fluctuating course over aperiod of hours to days. Individuals with delirium frequently have significant changes in their affective modulation as well, and may be angry or irritable, apathetic or disinterested, or manic-like and high, with rapid shifts in mood. Not uncommonly patients with delirium become quite agitated at night, and may reverse their sleep/wake cycle, sleeping only during the day. Of interest, findings on the electroencephalogram (EEG) of individuals with delirium show generalized slowing over the cerebral cortex. Also of interest, delirium may develop in as many as 10–20% of patients over age 65 who are hospitalized for medical illness.

Delirium may develop in the context of specific medical illnesses (for example hepatic encephalopathy or liver failure, and in response to various medications), but often develops in a context where there are multiple possible contributing factors, such as in the current case.

The management of delirium generally involves attempting to ascertain the specific cause or causes and if possible reversing them (for example, if there is an infection present, treating it with antibiotics; if a drug is causing the delirium, withdrawing the drug). Patients with delirium need to be carefully managed in that they may injure themselves in their confused state. They often require constant one-on-one supervision and at times will need to be restrained for their own protection. Many times they are treated with antipsychotic drugs that seem to suppress the delirium and allow the patient to get much needed rest. However, the specific underlying etiology should be aggressively sought.

A diagnosis to be excluded in differential diagnosis is dementia. Both disorders are characterized by memory impairment. Patients with dementia usually do not have the marked disturbance in level of consciousness that is seen with delirium, and the symptoms usually develop gradually and are progressive in their development rather than abrupt and severe.

☐ Questions for Further Discussion

1) What laboratory tests or other diagnostic procedures should be undertaken at this point to ascertain the cause of Mr. Jeffries' disorder?
2) Delirium is far more likely to develop in the elderly. Why?
3) What could the nurses do to help the patient tolerate his current condition and minimize his distress?

☐ References

American Psychiatric Association. (1994). *Diagnostic and statistical manual of mental disorders* (4th ed.). Washington, DC: Author.

☐ Suggested Readings

Chan, D., & Brennan, N. J. (1999). Delirium: Making the diagnosis, improving the prognosis. *Geriatrics, 54,* 28–30, 36, 39–42.

Flacker, J. M., & Marcantonio, E. R. (1998). Delirium in the elderly. Optimal management. *Drugs and Aging, 13,* 119–130.

Hassan, E., Fontaine, D. K., & Nearman, H. S. (1998). Therapeutic considerations in the management of agitated or delirious critically ill patients. *Pharmacotherapy, 18,* 113–129.

Inouye, S. K. (1998). Delirium in hospitalized older patients. *Clinical Geriatric Medicine, 14,* 745–764.

Inouye, S. K., Schlesinger, M. J., & Lydon, T. J. (1999). Delirium: A symptom of how hospital care is failing older persons and a window to improve quality of hospital care. *American Journal of Medicine, 106,* 565–573.

Jacobson, S., & Schrebmann, B. (1997). Behavioral and pharmacologic treatment of delirium. *American Family Physician, 56,* 2005–2012.

Knopman, D. S. (1998). The initial recognition and diagnosis of dementia. *American Journal of Medicine, 104,* 2S–12S.

Meagher, D. J., & Trzepacz, P. T. (1998). Delirium phenomenology illuminates pathophysiology, management, and course. *Journal of Geriatric Psychiatry and Neurology, 11,* 150–158.

Meredith, R. E. (1998). Detecting delirium in hospitalized older people. *Professional Nurse, 13,* 760–763.

Trzepacz, P. T. (1999). The Delirium Rating Scale: Its use in consultation-liaison research. *Psychosomatics, 40,* 193–204.

van der Mast, R. C. (1998). Pathophysiology of delirium. *Journal of Geriatric Psychiatry Neurology, 11,* 138–45

Dementia of the Alzheimer's Type

☐ Introduction

Although different forms of dementia tend to present with the same or similar symptoms, there are many possible underlying etiologies, and it is frequently very difficult to ascertain the specific cause in a given patient except on post-mortem examination. For example, dementia can develop secondary to vascular disease in the brain, after head trauma, in association with Huntington's chorea, and in those infected with the HIV virus. There are also specific types of primary dementia, wherein no specific offending agent can be identified. These include Pick's disease and Alzheimer's disease. Alzheimer's tends to affect much of the brain while Pick's seems to focus primarily on the frontal and anterior temporal lobes.

The following scenarios illustrate dementia of the Alzheimer's type with a late onset (beyond age 65). In reading these stories, consider the following questions:

1) Are recent memory and remote memory (memory of things in the last few days versus things many years ago) differentially affected?
2) What would be the problems one would be confronted with if one lived with a relative who had Alzheimer's disease?

☐ Diagnostic Criteria
(DSM-IV)

A. The development of multiple cognitive deficits manifested by both:

1) Memory impairment (impaired ability to learn new information or to recall previously learned information)
2) One (or more) of the following cognitive disturbances:
   a) aphasia (language disturbance)
   b) apraxia (impaired ability to carry out motor activities despite intact motor function)
   c) agnosia (failure to recognize or identify objects despite intact sensory function)
   d) disturbance in executive functioning (i.e., planning, organizing, sequencing, abstracting)

B. The cognitive deficits in Criteria A1 and A2 each cause significant impairment in social or occupational functioning and represent a significant decline from a previous level of functioning.
C. The course is characterized by gradual onset and continuing cognitive decline.
D. The cognitive deficits in Criteria A1 and A2 are not due to any of the following:
   1) Other central nervous system conditions that cause progressive deficits in memory and cognition (e.g., cerebrovascular disease, Parkinson's disease, Huntington's disease, subdural hematoma, normal-pressure hydrocephalus, brain tumor).
   2) Systemic conditions that are known to cause dementia (e.g., hypothyroidism, vitamin B_{12} or folic acid deficiency, niacin deficiency, hypercalcemia, neurosyphilis, HIV infection).
   3) Substance-induced conditions.
E. The deficits do not occur exclusively during the course of delirium.
F. The disturbance is not better accounted for by another Axis I disorder (e.g., major depressive disorder, schizophrenia).

☐ The Stories

I

It was Saturday afternoon and Rick, Jr., age 15, had lots of things he would rather be doing than going with his father to the nursing home downtown to visit his grandfather. He knew his friends were shooting baskets at the park down the street from his home. He had protested, as usual, but his parents thought it important that he visit his grandfather at least once a month. It had now been six weeks that he had avoided going. Although it seemed to him like his grandfather had been in the nursing home forever, it had actually been five years, and when he tried he could still vaguely remember what his grandfather had been like before his illness. He recalled a tall, robust man, looking younger than his age, who loved his grandchildren and enjoyed taking them to the park in the summer or to movies at other times of the year. He recalled a visit to the Shrine Circus when he was eight, and the fun they had had together, although the clowns scared him. Things had started going downhill around the time his grandfather retired, and things had gotten steadily worse since. He really hated visiting the nursing home and seeing all the old people. The ward his grandfather was on was full of confused old people who didn't know what was going on. He found the place both scary and depressing. He hated the smell. He also found being around his grandfather frightening, ever since the episode about six months ago when for no apparent reason his grandfather had struck out at him, grabbing him by the arm and yelling profanities at him.

They parked in the lot adjacent to the home, entered through the side door, and took the elevator to the third floor, which was the "Alzheimer's Unit." They buzzed the nursing station to be let in through the locked door, and started down the hall, passing the nursing station and exchanging pleasantries with the young staff nurse on duty, before turning left into John Siever's room.

Mr. Seiver sat upright in the chair by the window with a flat, expressionless look on his face. He watched them as they entered the room, showing no evidence of recognition. He passively allowed his right hand to be picked up and shaken by his son. Rick, Jr. sat on the edge of the bed, his usual perch for such visits. Mr. Siever didn't seem to recognize either of them. Rick, Sr. had brought his father some magazines. He wasn't sure exactly why—they were never read—it just seemed like the thing to do. He placed the magazines on his father's lap. John Siever picked them up abstractly, gazed down at them, and didn't seem to know what they were or what to do with them, so Rick, Sr. took them back and laid them on the bed next to his son.

Mr. Siever seemed disinterested in his visitors and said nothing for the first 10 minutes or so they were there. Rick, Sr. found that these visits were often characterized by long silences. However, Mr. Seiver eventually turned to his son and said, "Would you tell Edna to come in here?" As Rick, Sr. knew only too well, this was frequently his father's request, despite the fact that Edna, his mother, had been dead now for 12 years, the victim of breast cancer in her late 50s. It always made him think about the depth of the bond between his father and mother when his father asked about her.

Rick, Sr. patted his father's shoulder gently and said, "Dad, why don't we go out to the park? We can get the wheelchair down the hall. It's a beautiful day, the sun's out, the flowers are in bloom, I think you'd really like it."

Mr. Seiver seemed disinterested or did not understand, and his son repeated the suggestion. Mr. Seiver replied by shaking his head no, turned to his right, and looked out the window into the park.

Ralph, a large man in his thirties, one of the nursing assistants, came into the room. He greeted Rick, Sr. and Rick, Jr., asked Rick, Jr. how the summer soccer season was going at school, and circled around behind Mr. Seiver's chair, patting him on the shoulder. "Hey John, why don't you go outside with your son and grandson. It is a beautiful day. I think it would be good for you to get out. You haven't been out of this room in weeks."

II

John Seiver looked around his room (This is not my house. I wonder where Edna is. Things have been so confusing lately. I wouldn't be so confused if Edna were here).

Two men came into the room and greeted him. One, a man of about 40, the other an adolescent boy. They both seemed friendly but he did not recognize either of them (Who are these people? Why are they here in my room? And why does this one call me Dad?). He turned to the older man and asks, "Would you tell Edna to come in here?" but the man didn't respond. John's mind wandered. He had such little energy, looking around the room tired him. (And what is this they put in my lap? Junk?) He really saw nothing that interested him. He had a vague sense of being hungry and wondered when the next meal would be. He had a warm feeling in his groin area, glanced down, and realized that he had wet himself (Oh well, I am starting to feel hungry. I wonder if Edna is fixing dinner?).

☐ Discussion

We have evidence that Mr. Seiver has multiple cognitive problems, including profound problems with memory. We also have evidence of agnosia (he fails to recognize the magazines for what they are). He clearly is markedly impaired by his illness, being in a nursing home. We have evidence that the illness has progressed for at least five years, and we have no evidence that some other disorder is responsible for the disorder. Although it isn't completely clear from the story when the disorder first appeared, it was probably around the age of 65.

Individuals with dementia can demonstrate a variety of emotional and cognitive abnormalities, including disorientation (not knowing where they are, when it is, or who they are), problems with visuospacial relationships (inability to copy drawings), lack of understanding or insight (not knowing that they are ill), and poor judgment (driving a car or cooking when they lack the capacity).

Brain imaging techniques such as computerized tomography or magnetic resonance imaging may be useful in revealing evidence of cerebral atrophy, which is often global in patients with Alzheimer's disease. Alzheimer's disease tends to develop late in life. In general, the older one is the higher the risk of developing this condition The course is progressive, with the individual eventually succumbing to infection or some other terminal event.

For the differential diagnosis, depression must always be excluded, since depression in the elderly can present as cognitive impairment. We must also remember that some modest cognitive decline, particularly in memory and for naming objects, occurs as a normal part of aging.

Treatment for the most part is symptomatic with much of the care focusing on the prevention of complications, and institutionalization is frequently required.

☐ Questions for Further Discussion

1) Given our aging population (the aging of the baby boomer generation and the fact that people in general are living longer) what are the implications for the health care of the elderly with dementia?
2) Who was Alzheimer? What other disorder did he research extensively prior to turning to dementia?
3) Why are "Alzheimer's Units" created?

☐ References

American Psychiatric Association. (1994). *Diagnostic and statistical manual of mental disorders* (4th ed.). Washington, DC: author.

☐ Suggested Readings

Boller, F., & Forbes, M. M. (1998). History of dementia and dementia in history: An overview. *Journal of Neurological Sciences, 158,* 125–133.

Borson, S., & Raskind, M. A. (1997). Clinical features and pharmacologic treatment of behavioral symptoms of Alzheimer's disease. *Neurology, 48,* S17–S24.

Felician, O., & Sandson, T. A. (1999). The neurobiology and pharmacotherapy of Alzheimer's disease. *Journal of Neuropsychiatry and Clinical Neuroscience, 11,* 19–31.

Fleischman, D. A., & Gabrieli, J. (1999). Long-term memory in Alzheimer's disease. *Current Opinion in Neurobiology, 9,* 240–244.

Flynn, B. L. (1999). Pharmacologic management of Alzheimer's disease. Part 1: Hormonal and emerging investigational drug therapies. *Annuals of Pharmacotherapy, 33,* 178–187.

Francis, P. T., Palmer, A. M., Snape, M., & Wilcock, G. K. (1999). The cholinergic hypothesis of Alzheimer's disease: A review of progress. *Journal of Neurology, Neurosurgery and Psychiatry, 66,* 137–147.

Gauthier, S. (1999). Do we have a treatment for Alzheimer's disease? Yes. *Archives of Neurology, 56,* 738–739.

Growdon, J. H. (1999). Biomarkers of Alzheimer's disease. *Archives of Neurology, 56,* 281–283.

Hecker, J. (1998). Alzheimer's disease: The advent of effective therapy. *Australian and New Zealand Journal of Medicine, 28,* 765–771.

Martin, J. B. (1999). Molecular basis of the neurodegenerative disorders. *New England Journal of Medicine, 340,* 1970–1980.

Mohs, R. C. (1996). The Alzheimer's Disease Assessment Scale. *International Journal of Psychogeriatrics, 8,* 195–203.

Pasquier, F. (1999), Early diagnosis of dementia: Neuropsychology. *Journal of Neurology, 246,* 6–15.

Pryse-Phillips, W. (1999). Do we have drugs for dementia? No. *Archives of Neurology, 56,* 735–777.

Richards, S. S., & Hendrie, H. C. (1999). Diagnosis, management, and treatment of Alzheimer's disease: A guide for the internist. *Archives of Internal Medicine, 159,* 789–798.

Salek, S. S., Walker, M. D., & Bayer, A. J. (1998). A review of quality of life in Alzheimer's disease. Part 2: Issues in assessing drug effects. *Pharmacoeconomics, 14,* 613–627.

Scheltens, P. (1999), Early diagnosis of dementia: Neuroimaging. *Journal of Neurology, 246,* 16–20.

Seabrook, G. R., & Rosahl, T. W. (1999). Transgenic animals relevant to Alzheimer's disease. *Neuropharmracology, 38,* 1–17.

Small, G. W., & Leiter, F. (1998). Neuroimaging for diagnosis of dementia. *Journal of Clinical Psychiatry, 59,* 4–7.

van Reekum, R., Black, S. E., Conn, D., & Clarke, D. (1997). Cognition-enhancing drugs in dementia: A guide to the near future. *Canadian Journal of Psychiatry, 42,* 35S–50S.

Whitehouse, P. J. (1997). Pharmacoeconomics of dementia. *Alzheimer Disease and Associate Disorders, 11,* S22–S33.

II

SUBSTANCE RELATED DISORDERS

In the DSM-IV this section focuses on the intoxication with, abuse of, and/or dependence on drugs of abuse. Such drugs may include alcohol, sedative/hypnotics such as benzodiazepines, amphetamines, and other psychostimulants (e.g., speed), cannabis (e.g., marijuana), hallucinogens (e.g., LSD), inhalants (e.g., gasoline), and opioids (e.g., heroin), as well as phencyclidine (PCP), caffeine, and nicotine. To illustrate all the various drugs, and the various levels of use and abuse possible with each individually, as well as with their combinations, would require many stories indeed. Instead, I have chosen two drugs to discuss: alcohol dependence and amphetamine dependence.

Alcohol Dependence

☐ Introduction

Alcohol dependence is characterized by the excessive use of alcohol to the point that the body becomes physically dependent on the drug, as evidenced by symptoms of tolerance (needing to use larger amounts of the drug to get the same effect) or withdrawal (an adverse physical reaction upon discontinuation). Alcohol dependence is by far the most common form of dependence on drugs of abuse, and represents a massive public health concern. It occurs more often in men than in women, thus our "story" concerns a man. In the scenario that follows, consider the following issues:

1) Notice the bargaining that goes on in John's mind, and his profound ambivalence about giving up the alcohol.
2) What effects is his drinking having on his family?
3) Dorothy clearly wasn't aware that this was a problem. Do you think hidden alcohol abuse and dependence are common?

☐ Diagnostic Criteria
(DSM-IV)

A. A maladaptive pattern of substance use, leading to clinically significant impairment or distress, as manifested by three (or more) of the following, occurring at any time in the same 12-month period:

1) Tolerance, as defined by either of the following:
    a) a need for markedly increased amounts of the substance to achieve intoxication or desired effect
    b) markedly diminished effect with continued use of the same amount of the substance
2) Withdrawal, as manifested by either of the following:
    a) the characteristic withdrawal syndrome for the substance
    b) the same (or a closely related) substance is taken to relieve or avoid withdrawal symptoms
3) The substance is often taken in larger amounts or over a longer period than was intended.
4) There is a persistent desire or unsuccessful efforts to cut down or control substance use.
5) A great deal of time is spent in activities necessary to obtain the substance (e.g., visiting multiple doctors or driving long distances), use the substance (e.g., chain-smoking), or recover from its effects.
6) Important social, occupational, or recreational activities are given up or reduced because of substance use.
7) The substance use is continued despite knowledge of having a persistent or recurrent physical or psychological problem that is likely to have been caused or exacerbated by the substance (e.g., current cocaine use despite recognition of cocaine-induced depression, or continued drinking despite recognition that an ulcer was made worse by alcohol consumption).

☐ The Stories

I

Helen Nezbit's mother, Dorothy, grey haired but looking much younger than her fifty odd years was waiting expectantly for Helen at the gate. When Helen and her seven year old son, Jack, disembarked from the plane, Dorothy could see that Helen was tired and played out. Dorothy had been heartsick and worried ever since she had gotten her daughter's call the night before telling her that Helen was leaving her husband, John, and coming with Jack to stay with her.

Dorothy and Helen hugged warmly, and kissed each other's cheek. Dorothy hugged Jack, who appeared tired and preoccupied, and they started down the airport concourse to collect the luggage. Later in the car on the way to Dorothy's home, Dorothy couldn't contain her concern any longer, "What's happened between you and John?" Helen replied that she preferred not to talk about it in front of her son, and that perhaps when they got to Dorothy's house and put Jack to bed they could talk about it then. They spent the rest of the car trip in silence.

Later that evening, after Jack had fallen asleep on the couch in the den and had been carried to bed by his mother, Helen and Dorothy sat down at the kitchen table to talk over coffee.

Helen began slowly, tearing up as she did, "Mother, I should have told you about this a long time ago, or told somebody about it, but I simply can't stand it anymore. John's an alcoholic and he won't get help."

Dorothy was flabbergasted, "An alcoholic? I know he is a heavy drinker but so was your father."

"No mother, not a heavy drinker, an alcoholic. John has been drinking every day for years now. It used to be just in the evenings. Sometimes he would stop for a beer, or probably several beers, on the way home, have a drink before dinner, then pour a very large drink after dinner. Vodka usually, sometimes gin. I used to think it wasn't much but then I started watching. Recently he's gotten to the point where he's drinking about a fifth of liquor a day. For the last year I've been finding empty bottles around the house. He hides them places. He hides them in his dresser drawers, he hides them in the basement. I think he keeps one in his car. I don't think a night has gone by in the last year when John wasn't drunk when he went to bed. He spends almost no time with Jack. Jack doesn't even try to get John to play with him anymore because he knows that Jack is always "busy," or asleep. His moods are all over the place. Sometimes he seems happy and other times, right after, he seems depressed. Physically he looks like hell. His face is flushed all the time, he's put on weight, he doesn't get any exercise at all.

"It's like I don't exist. It's like he's in his own little world and Jack and I aren't part of it. I can't take it any longer. I can't even talk to him most of the time. He's not really part of my life anymore. He's in his own world. He's going to kill himself with the drinking."

"Can't he get help? Can't he go to AA or one of those treatment programs? They advertise them all the time on T.V."

"He talks about it when I get angry with him, but then other times he says that our insurance won't cover it, or he doesn't have time, or it wouldn't work anyway. I simply don't know what I'm going to do, but last night when I saw him drunk and asleep on the couch, the T.V. blaring in the background at 8:00 in the evening, I said 'This is it. I'm leaving,' and called you."

II

It was 5:00 p.m. Saturday and John Nesbit was on his way home. The drive would take about 20 minutes. The men's store where he worked had just closed. He hated to work Saturdays but it was part of the job.

Helen had been back from her mother's now for three days. A week ago she had run off with Jack, their son, angry as hell and not willing to listen to reason, and had blown a bunch of money on expensive plane tickets, only to return home after a few days. He had said, sure, I won't drink any longer, and if he did he would get treatment. He realized that it had become something of a problem, and expensive, too. If he stopped to think about it, the whole thing was crazy, sitting around watching T.V., drinking, ignoring his wife and son. Hell, ignoring everything, but it was the only way he could relax. Doesn't she understand that? He works hard to support his family and deserves just to be able to "come down." When he drank he could feel it right away. He had learned now to take a big drink to start with so he would "get mellow" in 10 or 15 minutes. The problem was that it didn't last long enough and he had to drink more to keep that feeling. Pretty soon you were talking funny and couldn't remember anything, and couldn't walk straight.

He had always liked drinking. He had loved to "party" in college, and had actually dropped out in his junior year. His wife, Helen, had been his steady girl in college. She went on to finish her degree and was now a teacher. They had stuck together all these years, although she harped at him all the time now about his drinking. Their relationship was going to hell. Well, he'd show her. He hadn't had a drink now in four days. He wasn't sure he was going to quit forever. He thought maybe the best approach would be to go back to being a social drinker—maybe allow himself one or two drinks in the evening. Maybe that would be the best plan. Or, maybe he should allow himself one night a week when he could drink as much as he wanted. Maybe Saturday night would work well. She would have to be satisfied with that, then he wouldn't get into any trouble, then he could do more things with Jack on the other nights and more things with Helen.

Just briefly he thought back to his own childhood, to his father, Barry, a construction worker and a heavy drinker. They hadn't done much together. Barry was usually gone somewhere with his friends. When he would come back he was often drunk and mean. John had never been mean to anyone. He had never hit Helen or Jack; therefore, he didn't have a problem like his father.

Turning south onto Lombard he remembered that Stan Lansing's house was a couple of blocks down on the right. Stan would be sitting in the living room drinking a beer and watching the football game. He hadn't seen Stan in weeks and it would be great to see him. Maybe some of the other guys would be there, too. He'd only drink beer. That wouldn't cause any problems.

☐ Discussion

In this scenario we have evidence that John has developed a tolerance to alcohol (he is now drinking a fifth of liquor a day). There seems to be desire and effort to cut down or control his use, but he has been unsuccessful. Clearly, his drinking is having a marked impact on his functioning as a father and his relationship with his wife. Therefore, criteria for substance dependence are met.

Misuse of alcohol in our culture is very common, and the majority of men at some point in their life will engage at least briefly in drinking that is problematic for them (e.g., they will miss work because of a hangover), but most do not develop an ongoing pattern of abuse or develop symptoms of dependence. However, alcohol dependence is surprisingly common, and is about twice as common among men as women.

Some experts categorize male alcohol abusers into two main groups. The first group is an early onset group wherein drinking becomes a problem in adolescence or young adulthood. These individuals often engage in binge drinking, and usually have a strong family history of alcohol abuse. They also are likely to have problems with antisocial personality. The second group is a later onset group of individuals who gradually develop drinking problems over time. Family history of alcohol abuse is less common here, and these individuals are generally older, better established occupationally and socially, and more responsive to treatment.

Alcohol is toxic to many organ systems and it is not uncommon for people with alcohol dependence to eventually develop medical complications of the illness. These may frequently include gastrointestinal problems (hepatitis or other liver problems, pancreatitis or inflammation of the pancreas), and neurological problems (memory problems, and, in a subset, dementia). Withdrawal tremor can occur, and in about 5% of cases withdrawal can progress to delirium tremens (so called DTs) where there is a disturbed level of consciousness, autonomic hyperactivity, and risk of death).

These days alcohol treatment is usually conducted in outpatient facilities. Different models are used including the Alcoholics Anonymous model, and cognitive behavioral treatment. Alcoholic Anonymous groups are widely available to offer support and help to people with alcohol abuse problems. Recently there has been interest in using a medication, Naltrexone, to prevent relapse in those recovering from alcohol dependence. The drug seems to decrease cravings for alcohol, making it more likely for people to be able to abstain from drinking .

Once a pattern of alcohol dependence has been established, it is highly unlikely that individuals will be able to go back to a pattern of social drinking after treatment, and most seem to need to remain abstinent indefinitely.

☐ Questions for Further Discussion

1) Those with alcohol dependence are at higher risk for premature death from a number of causes. What are these causes?
2) The rate of alcohol dependence appears to be higher in the United States than in most western industrialized societies. Why?
3) A growing literature suggests a strong heritability or genetic diathesis for alcoholism. What sort of traits or characteristics might be inherited that would make one at higher risk for developing alcohol abuse/dependence problems?

☐ References

American Psychiatric Association. (1994). *Diagnostic and statistical manual of mental disorders* (4th ed.). Washington, DC: Author.

☐ Suggested Readings

Buck, K. J. (1998). Recent progress toward the identification of genes related to risk for alcoholism. *Mammalian Genome, 9*, 927–928.

Burge, S. K., & Schneider, F. D. (1999). Alcohol-related problems: Recognition and intervention. *American Family Physician, 59*, 361–370.

Deehan, A., Marshall, E. J., & Strang, J. (1998). Tackling alcohol misuse: Opportunities and obstacles in primary care. *British Journal of General Practice, 48*, 1779–1782.

Finfgeld, D. L. (1999). Use of brief interventions to treat individuals with drinking problems. *Journal of Psychosocial Nursing and Mental Health Services, 37*, 23–30.

Lepine, J. P., & Pelissolo, A. (1998). Social phobia and alcoholism: A complex relationship. *Journal of Affective Disorders, 50*, S23–S28

Lesch, O. M., & Walter, H. (1996). New "state" markers for the detection of alcoholism. *Alcohol and Alcoholism, Supplement, 1*, 59–62.

Lynskey, M. T. (1998). The comorbidity of alcohol dependence and affective disorders: Treatment implications. *Drug and Alcohol Dependencies, 52*, 201–209.

McGinnis, J. M., & Foege, W. H. (1999). Mortality and morbidity attributable to use of addictive substances in the United States. *Proceedings of the Association of American Physicians, 111,* 109–118.

Raimo, E. B., & Schuckit, M. A. (1998). Alcohol dependence and mood disorders. *Addictive Behaviors, 23,* 933–946.

Rosalki, S. B. (1999). Biochemical identification of alcohol abuse. *International Journal of Clinical Practice, 53,* 138–139.

Schaffer, A., & Naranjo, C. A. (1998). Recommended drug treatment strategies for the alcoholic patient. *Drugs, 56,* 571–585.

Swift, R. M. (1999). Drug therapy for alcohol dependence. *New England Journal of Medicine, 3340,* 1482–1490.

CHAPTER 4

Amphetamine Dependence

☐ Introduction

The following scenarios detail amphetamine dependence in an adolescent male. The term "amphetamines" describes a variety of drugs, all of which have basic phenylethylamine structure. These include drugs such as methamphetamine, dextramphetamine, and amphetamine itself. Sometimes these are referred to as "diet drugs," although they are rarely used for that purpose anymore. Although there are medically approved uses for amphetamines (e.g., narcolepsy or certain cases of attention deficit hyperactivity disorder), their abuse liability has dictated that clinicians usually prescribe drugs with relatively weak amphetamine effects (and less abuse liability), like methylphenidate. The effects of amphetamines are similar to the effects of cocaine in that they cause stimulation, hyperactivity, and can mimic psychosis.

In reading the following examples, consider the following points:

1) Notice the change in pattern of usage over time, from recreational to daily use, with an accompanying change in tolerance.
2) What are the psychosocial consequences of amphetamine abuse for this individual? How is it affecting school work? Relationships? Self-esteem? Athletic ability?
3) Is amphetamine intoxication as obvious to other people as alcohol intoxication?

☐ Diagnostic Criteria

(DSM-IV)

A. A maladaptive pattern of substance use, leading to clinically significant impairment or distress, as manifested by three (or more) of the
following, occurring at any time in the same 12-month period:

1) Tolerance, as defined by either of the following:
   a) a need for markedly increased amounts of the substance to
   achieve intoxication or desired effect.
   b) markedly diminished effect with continued use of the same
   amount of the substance.
2) Withdrawal, as manifested by either of the following:
   a) the characteristic withdrawal syndrome for the substance (refer
   to Criteria A and B of the criteria sets for Withdrawal from
   the specific substances)
   b) the same (or a closely related) substance is taken to relieve
   or avoid withdrawal symptoms.
3) The substance is often taken in larger amounts or over a longer
   period than was intended.
4) There is a persistent desire or unsuccessful efforts to cut down
   or control substance use.
5) A great deal of time is spent in activities necessary to obtain the
   substance (e.g., visiting multiple doctors or driving long distances), use the substance (e.g., chain smoking), or recover from
   its effects.
6) Important occupational, or recreational activities are given up
   or reduced because of substance use.
7) The substance use is continued despite knowledge of having a
   persistent or recurrent physical or psychological problem that
   is likely to have been caused or exacerbated by the substance
   (e.g., current cocaine use despite recognition of cocaine-induced
   depression, or continued drinking despite recognition that an
   ulcer was made worse by alcohol consumption).

☐ The Stories

I

Brett had tried to quit before. During the summer he had gone camping alone (something his parents had actively discouraged) with a
plan of "drying out" over a period of four or five days and breaking

the habit. He felt his resolve start to waiver as he was driving up to the state park to camp, and soon after pitching his tent and fixing his dinner, the craving started to grow. He had been there for less than six hours before he was in the car and driving to Scott's house to score some speed.

Brett was well aware that he had a problem. He could still remember that Saturday night about eight months before when his friend Scott had introduced him to "white crosses." Scott and Brett had spent most of that afternoon playing basketball. After dinner Brett was exhausted and Scott said he had something that would get him going. Brett had experimented with other drugs before. He had tried marijuana on several occasions, and cocaine once. He found the cocaine exhilarating but hadn't had access to it again. Now he had unlimited access to amphetamines. Scott was willing to supply him with all he needed, although it was expensive. At first he thought it was well worth it, but now he wasn't so sure.

As a junior in high school, growing up in a small Montana town, Brett had been a standout point guard on the basketball team. He consistently scored in double figures, but really hadn't been playing well lately. He made stupid mistakes including missed shots and bad passes. The day before he was called for a foul and he stomped away from the referee in a disrespectful manner, and later was called for a foul when he pushed another player under the basket. He had been pulled from the game by his coach.

While at first he had only used speed once or twice a week for fun, he found he was now using it daily, often taking it when he got up in the morning as a way to jump start the day. He found that if he didn't take it he was paralyzed with lack of energy, and the world seemed black and dark, but when he was high things were great. He seemed to have limitless energy. He seemed to be able to think so clearly and concentrate on things. It seemed his memory was better, that he would fly through tasks, although at times he would become preoccupied with things that later seemed trivial. For example, one night he had rearranged all the books in the house (a sizeable number given his father's interest in book collecting). Sometimes he became preoccupied with the idea of figuring out how things worked. He had spent hours taking apart a computer that was outdated and no longer used, stored in the family basement. He had never been able to get it back together and hoped that his parents would never find it.

When he started out he would use only one or two pills, but now it usually took five to ten to get the same effect. The habit was getting expensive. His father, Ralph Phillips, also collected antique watches and Brett had taken one and sold it to have money for the drugs. He had also started taking money out of his mother's purse when there was enough there that he thought she wouldn't notice.

He realized he had to stop, but he really couldn't see how. Things were so out of control. At times in the blackness when he found the drugs wearing off he began to wish he were dead as a way of ending the problem.

His mother and father had sat him down and talked to him about things on two occasions. They had noticed his moodiness and that he didn't seem to study as he had before. Was he having academic problems?

II

Brett's coach, Dale Andrews, told him he wanted him to stay after practice. Brett was to shower, dress, and meet him in his office. Brett was sure that the coach was upset with him after the game two days before, and wasn't looking forward to the meeting. Practice ended at 4:30 and 15 minutes later he was seated in the coach's office across his desk in the straight back wooden chair that players always sat in when being talked to.

"Brett, I don't know what's going on, but it's not good. You haven't been playing well for weeks. Very erratic. Sometimes you seem to really cruise while at other times you shoot when you shouldn't—I mean really bad air balls—and make stupid passes. The other guys are starting to not pass to you. Have you noticed that? Also, you've been losing weight. You were never a big kid but now you look skinny. People are going to push you around on the court. Also, you are a pain to be around. You get mad at stupid little things. I saw the way you pushed that player during the game and I couldn't believe how you reacted to that ref."

"You're right coach, I've been making some mistakes lately. I'll work on it."

"Brett, it's not that easy. I've talked to some of your other teachers about it. Everybody says you're having problems. Is something going on at home?"

"Oh no. Things are fine at home. Things are fine."

"I'm going to have to talk to the assistant principal about this. I think we need to have a meeting with your parents. I think something is wrong and we've got to figure out what it is."

Brett abruptly got up out of his chair, shoved it backward, and stomped out of the room. Mr. Andrews called after him, "Brett, wait, I'm not done talking to you."

Brett yelled as he went through the door, "Yes, you are," and in a fit of anger marched down the hall to his locker. He fumbled, tremulous and shaky, with the combination lock. He opened the door of his locker, dumped in his books, and slammed the locker shut. He then left school, proceeded to jump in his car (a used junker he had saved up for by working the prior summer), and pounded his fists into the steering wheel. He looked into the rearview mirror, saw his angry reddened face. He reached under the driver seat and extracted a baggy which contained several dozen pills of various colors. He shook out six "white crosses," popped them in his mouth, and washed them down with the residual soda in a can in the backseat floor. (At this point it doesn't matter if they kick me out of school. To hell with it. I'm out of here.) He started the car and squealing the tires, swerved out of the student parking lot and onto the highway.

☐ Discussion

In reviewing this case, the criteria for substance dependence appear to have been met. We have evidence of tolerance, withdrawal when the substance is not taken, using the substance in increasingly large amounts, unsuccessful attempts to discontinue the use of the substance, spending time in activities to obtain the substance, reduction in important, social, occupational, or recreational activities, and continued use of the substance despite knowledge of having had persistent psychological problems because of the use (such as depression). This is a fairly typical, straightforward example of the development of substance dependence occurring in an adolescent.

Amphetamine abuse can sometimes be confused with psychotic illnesses such as schizophrenia or schizophreniform disorder. The individual in the current case does not appear to have developed psychotic symptoms and, therefore, these alternative diagnoses would be easily ruled out.

The clinical picture is very close to what one would see in someone with cocaine abuse, and it is important to establish that this individual is not abusing cocaine or other substances as well as amphetamine. Some of his symptoms are suggestive of mania (e.g., hyperactivity), but the clear history of amphetamine intake confirms the amphetamine abuse diagnosis (which could be confirmed by drug testing).

Amphetamine dependence is more common in men than women and most likely to occur during late adolescents and early adulthood. Although this individual ingested amphetamines orally, some amphetamine abusers administer drugs intravenously and, in the case of methamphetamine, nasally.

Various patterns of abuse can be seen. The one illustrated here is regular daily use. Another pattern is using speed in binges where the use is more sporadic, but during periods of administration binges may continue for several days. The development of depressive symptoms on withdrawal commonly occurs following a period of amphetamine abuse.

Medical complications of acute amphetamine intoxication are relatively rare. However, because these drugs tend to raise blood pressure and pulse, irregular heart rhythms or cardiac arrhythmias, and hypertensive episodes may develop in those at risk for these complications, particularly those with pre-existing hypertension or cardiac irregularities.

Individuals who use amphetamines intravenously, or any drugs intravenously, are at risk for a variety of other complications. These include exposure to the AIDS virus (through contaminated needles), the risk of hepatitis (five variants of which have now been identified), the development of abscesses in skin or soft tissue at the sight of administration, and infection of the heart called bacterial endocarditis, which can prove fatal. Because of this, intravenous drug users need to be carefully evaluated medically.

The treatment of amphetamine abuse and dependence is similar to the treatment of other substance abuse. The first step is discontinuation of usage, managing the individual through the difficult period of withdrawal, and intense psychoeducational treatment around issues of abuse and dependence. Many amphetamine abusers are treated in traditional Alcoholics Anonymous-type programs, although increasingly alternative formats—including cognitive behavioral treatment—of substance abuse are coming to the fore. Amphetamine abuse, as with most types of substance abuse, usually occurs in the context of the administration of multiple drugs, and is not easily treated. There is a substantial relapse rate in the first six months after treatment.

☐ Questions for Further Discussion

1) Given that amphetamine abusers can develop psychotic symptoms (delusions, hallucinations), and have a propensity toward attacks of anger, what are the risks of the abuse of this drug concerning possible violence?

2) If Brett had been your friend in high school, what could you have done to help him?

3) How do you think the basketball coach, and the school in general, should deal with Brett?

☐ References

American Psychiatric Association. (1994). *Diagnostic and statistical manual of mental disorders* (4th ed.). Washington, DC: Author.

☐ Suggested Readings

Buffenstein, A., Heaster, J., & Ko, P. (1999). Chronic psychotic illness from methamphetamine. *American Journal of Psychiatry, 156,* 662.

Churchill, A. C., Burgess, P. M., Pead, J., & Gill, T. (1993). Measurement of the severity of amphetamine dependence. *Addiction, 88,* 1335–1340.

Czerwinski, W. P. (1999), Amphetamine-related disorders. *Journal of Louisiana State Medical Society, 160,* 491–499.

Karch, S. (1999). The problem of methamphetamine toxicity. *Western Journal of Medicine, 170,* 232.

McKetin, R., & Mattick, R. P. (1998). Attention and memory in illicit amphetamine users: Comparison with non-drug using controls. *Drug and Alcohol Dependence, 50,* 181–184.

Murray, J. B. (1998). Psychophysiological aspects of amphetamine-methamphetamine abuse. *Journal of Psychology, 132,* 227–237.

Richards, J. R., Bretz, S. W., Johnson, E. B., Turnipseed, S. D., Brofeldt, B. T., & Derlet, R. W. (1999). Methamphetamine abuse and emergency department utilizatioin. *Western Journal Medicine, 170,* 198–202.

Ropero-Miller, J. D., & Goldberger, B. A. (1998). Recreational drugs. Current trends in the 90s. *Clinical Laboratory Medicine, 18,* 727–746.

Topp, L., & Darke, S. (1997). The applicability of the dependence syndrome to amphetamine. *Drug and Alcohol Dependence, 48,* 113–118.

PART

III

SCHIZOPHRENIA AND OTHER PSYCHOTIC DISORDERS

The title of this category is a bit misleading in that psychotic symptoms may be present in disorders outside of this grouping. However, psychotic features do characterize all of these illnesses. This leads us to the question: What does psychotic mean? Various definitions have been used over time. The DSM-IV offers different levels of definition, from a very narrow approach (prominent delusions and hallucinations with lack of insight), to a much broader one (causing gross impairment). In our discussion we will focus on the more narrow use of the term.

In the stories that follow I illustrate two forms of these disorders: schizophrenia and delusional disorder. These two were chosen since they in some sense represent the ends of a spectrum. Schizophrenia is characterized as causing gross impairment; in delusional disorder the symptoms are usually fairly circumscribed, and many individuals with this disorder function reasonably well. Not illustrated are schizophreniform disorder (a schizophrenia-appearing disorder that lasts less than six months but more than one month), schizoaffective disorder (wherein one sees a mixture of mood disturbance and schizophrenic symptomatology), brief psychotic disorder (which remits within a month), and shared psychotic disorder (which used to be known as Folie à Deux, an interesting phenomena where two isolated individuals both become delusional. One is actually ill and convinces the other person of the delusion). There are also categories for psychotic disorder secondary to substance and medical conditions, as well as the usual catch-all "not otherwise specified."

At the outset it is important to stress that these disorders are common and quite serious, with schizophrenia being one of the most disabling conditions of all psychiatric disorders.

Schizophrenia

☐ Introduction

Schizophrenia is a severe psychotic disorder characterized by a mixture of certain symptoms, some of which are referred to as positive or productive (e.g., hallucinations) and others as negative (e.g., withdrawal, anhedonia). Schizophrenia tends to be a devastating illness for affected individuals and for their families. It strikes people early in life during late adolescence or young adulthood, and lasts the remainder of the person's life, significantly attenuating their ability to function productively in society.

In reading the following stories, consider the following questions:

1) What has the time course of this illness been? How has it progressed?
2) This individual has some specific paranoid ideas. What are they?
3) How has this illness affected John's relationships with family members?

☐ Diagnostic Criteria
(DSM-IV)

A. *Characteristic symptoms:* Two (or more) of the following, each present for a significant portion of time during a 1-month period (or less if successfully treated):
1) Delusions
2) Hallucinations
3) Disorganized speech (e.g., frequent derailment or incoherence)

4) Grossly disorganized or catatonic behavior
5) Negative symptoms, i.e., affective flattening, alogia, or avolition
   Note: Only one Criterion A symptom is required if delusions are bizarre or hallucinations consist of a voice keeping up a running commentary on the person's behavior or thoughts, or two or more voices conversing with each other.

B. *Social/occupational dysfunction:* For a significant portion of the time since the onset of the disturbance, one or more major areas of functioning such as work, interpersonal relations, or self-care are markedly below the level achieved prior to the onset (or when the onset is in childhood or adolescence, failure to achieve expected level of interpersonal, academic, or occupational achievement).

C. *Duration:* Continuous signs of the disturbance persist for at least 6 months. This 6-month period must include at least 1 month of symptoms (or less if successfully treated) that meet Criterion A (i.e., active-phase symptoms) and may include periods of prodromal or residual symptoms. During these prodromal or residual periods, the signs of the disturbance may be manifested by only negative symptoms or two or more symptoms listed in Criterion A present in an attenuated form (e.g., odd beliefs, unusual perceptual experiences).

D. *Schizoaffective and Mood Disorder exclusion:* Schizoaffective Disorder and Mood Disorder With Psychotic Features have been ruled out because either: 1) no Major Depressive, Manic, or Mixed Episodes have occurred concurrently with the active-phase symptoms; or 2) if mood episodes have occurred during active-phase symptoms, their total duration has been brief relative to the duration of the active and residual periods.

E. *Substance/general medical condition exclusion:* The disturbance is not due to the direct physiological effects of a substance (e.g., a drug of abuse, a medication) or a general medical condition.

F. *Relationship to a Pervasive Developmental Disorder:* If there is a history of Autistic Disorder or another Pervasive Developmental Disorder, the additional diagnosis of Schizophrenia is made only if prominent delusions or hallucinations are also present for at least a month (or less if successfully treated).

☐ The Stories

I

It was spring—early May—and the grass and shrubs that ringed the screened-in porch had already attained that iridescent green that always fades by July or August. It was cool but comfortable on the porch. John's parents, Ralph and Joan, had been anticipating Wendy's visit home from college with mixed feelings. They naturally wanted to see her but knew that they could no longer hide from her the terrible concern that had slowly but inexorably now come to dominate their lives. They didn't know how to start, and Wendy helped by speaking first.

"Okay you guys, I know something's wrong and you need to tell me what it is. I've been able to tell every time I've talked to you on the phone for the last few weeks, and I'm a big kid now, in case you haven't noticed, and I need to know. I'm tired of being told 'nothing is wrong.' Is one of you sick?" Joan, then, felt even more of a burden. In addition to everything else, she had made Wendy worry for their physical health (Perhaps we should have told her earlier. Oh well, water under the bridge.)

"No, No, Wendy. We're both fine. It's not that. It's John. We're very worried about John and we don't know what to do." Joan disengaged from Wendy's gaze and fixed on the floor at her feet. Ralph, after all these years, knew this sign and realized that if he let her keep talking she would begin to cry.

"No Wendy, your mother and I are just fine. John, however, is not fine."

Wendy filled the silence of his pause. "Dad, John has always been a problem. As we've talked about, John has always been weird. He's just different. He always has been and I think he will always be, although you and mom always talked about him growing out of it. Anyway, what has he done? Has he gotten into trouble?"

Joan, her composure temporarily reestablished, leveled her gaze once again at her daughter.

"John is doing nothing. He hasn't gotten into trouble. He hasn't gotten into anything. For the last month he has been living in the basement. He has moved down there. He put up the camping cot in the corner, took down his sleeping bag, and hasn't slept in his room since."

Wendy was puzzled. "Why would he do that? Did he say why he did that?"

Ralph thought to himself, I have no idea why he does this or why he does anything, but said, "He won't talk to us. He says very little anymore. We hear him talking to himself sometimes in the basement at night."

Wendy questioned, "On the phone?"

Ralph continued, "No, he took the phone out. He says he doesn't want anything electrical near him. He said something about there being problems with the electricity. He also took the light bulbs out of the lamps in the basement. In the evening and at night it is black as pitch down there and he just sits there and smokes. He stays there. He lives there."

Questions whirled in Wendy's mind. "Well, what does he eat? Where does he go to the bathroom?"

Ralph continued, "He occasionally comes up and gets some food, but will never eat with us. He also doesn't cook. He just eats things raw, making himself a cheese sandwich or opening a can of spaghetti. Most of the time he takes it back downstairs. Sometimes he eats in the kitchen during the night. He comes up to use the bathroom in the hall but not very often. We think he probably urinates in the drain in the corner of the basement. It smells down there. He looks like hell."

"Well, he hasn't looked very good for years. He has that terrible beard and his hair is too long and he doesn't seem to care much about what he wears," answered Wendy.

Joan looked up again and tears brimmed over and began to silently run down her cheek. She spoke again in a soft voice, "He's much, much worse. He never combs his hair, he never washes his face, his clothes are filthy, he's so skinny I can't believe it."

II

John was thinking (I want a cigarette) as he lit one from his pack. He noticed that he only had four left. This was his second pack today. He would need more cigarettes. (I'll get them when I go to the kitchen. I need to wait until later, though. I heard mom and dad upstairs and I don't want to see them. They bug me too much. I just want to be left alone).

Things for the most part were quiet there, except for the voices. (I'm not sure where they come from, but they come in on the electric lines. I've taken apart the electrical fixtures here in the basement, but they're still getting in. I'm not sure who it is, but I think CIA. They would have the tools to do that sort of thing. The electricity. I'm not sure why they are after me. I wonder if they want me in the CIA. I'm not sure what I've done that makes them want me. Other than the voices, it's the insects that they blow in under the door or through the windows. There are so many insects down here but not much going on down here. I'd rather be left alone. There is the CIA voice again. The voice calling me an asshole. The voice telling me that the bugs are to bother me so that I'll go crazy.)

(This is the place for me to stay. I'm safest here. I want a cigarette.)

He lights a cigarette. (Why does the CIA use bugs? The bugs may be there to tell me something special. Maybe I'm special. I once had a .38 Special. Did the CIA take it)?

☐ Discussion

In considering these stories let us evaluate which of the diagnostic criteria are satisfied.

First, relative to characteristic symptoms, this individual appears to have delusions or false beliefs. Also, we have evidence of negative symptoms (his withdrawal to the basement, not doing things, not interacting with others). Clearly, his social/occupational functioning is impaired. He is out of work and his self-care skills have deteriorated as well. We have evidence that he may have been symptomatic for at least six months, although things have worsened lately. We don't have any evidence of an important mood component that would suggest a psychotic depression or schizoaffective disorder. We also have no evidence that his illness is substance induced or secondary to a medical condition, or that he has a history of autism or other pervasive developmental disorders.

In considering the diagnosis of schizophrenia, symptoms can be clustered into two groups, those referred to as positive and those referred to as negative. Positive symptoms generally represent distortion or at times exaggerations of what would be considered a normal phenomena while negative symptoms represent an absence or reduction in other normal phenomenon. Classically, positive symptoms include disorganized or unusual behavior, strange patterns of speech (characterized primarily by disorganization and rambling), hallucinations (or sensory perceptions for which there is no stimulus in the environment). Delusions, or false unshakable beliefs, are also common.

Behavioral abnormalities can vary dramatically and range from hyperactive behavior to complete lack of movement, a form of catatonia. The disorganization of speech can be subtle or severe and in some advanced cases it is very difficult to understand what the person is trying to say. Hallucinations can occur in any sensory modality (seeing, hearing, smelling, feeling, tasting), but most commonly are auditory.

Negative symptoms in DSM-IV focus on three specific patterns: poverty or lack of speech (referred to as alogia), lack of or narrowing of affective range (affective flattening), and lack of involvement in purposeful, goal-directed-behavior (avolition).

Schizophrenia can be subdivided into various subtypes including paranoid (prominent delusions and hallucinations), disorganized (marked disorganization in speech, behavior), catatonic type (marked changes in motor movements), as well as undifferentiated and residual. Schizophrenia must be differentiated from schizoaffective disorder (where the symptoms may be similar but the mood disturbance is prominent), and from more short lived psychotic processes (brief psychotic disorder, which remits within a month, and substance-induced psychotic disorders which generally remit when the person is no longer using the offending agent).

Schizophrenia generally develops in late adolescence or young adulthood. Most research suggests that the prevalence is approximately equal in males and females, although females tend to have a later age of onset and a better prognosis. The longitudinal course is highly variable and although some patients may improve with time, most remain ill, at least to some extent, for the remainder of their life, often with negative symptoms predominating at long-term follow-up. The prevalence of schizophrenia is about 1%, being far more common than many people realize. It is also highly heritable and siblings of patients with schizophrenia have a ten-fold increased risk of developing the disorder. Of interest, the concordance rate (both twins positive) among monozygotic (MZ) twins wherein one twin is affected (MZ twins being genetically identical) is only about 50%, and therefore other factors are undoubtedly involved, since someone can be genetically identical to someone with the disorder but not manifest it.

Although there are no laboratory tests that are specific for schizophrenia, many patients with schizophrenia evidence enlargement of the cerebral ventricles in brain imaging studies. Some also have what are called neurological soft signs indicating subtle neurological impairment.

The treatment of patients with schizophrenia is complex. It will frequently include supportive problem-oriented psychotherapy, as well as antipsychotic medication. In many cases much can be gained by working with caregivers involved in the patient's care. Antipsychotic medications have been shown to significantly suppress positive symptoms and frequently prevent the need for hospitalization. However, up until the last ten years most of the available agents had few effects on negative symptoms. This picture has changed dramatically in the last decade, and now several drugs are available that seem to improve negative symptoms as well. These new treatments have markedly improved treatment options for these patients. However, it is important to remember that these medications do not cure schizophrenia and most patients continue to have some residual symptoms that markedly impair their ability to function. In short, this is frequently a severe, debilitating illness.

☐ Questions for Further Discussion

1) Individuals with some psychiatric disorders are considered particularly gifted and insightful. Do you think this would be true of people with schizophrenia?
2) Give examples of additional possible delusions.
3) Is schizophrenia something we see only in industrialized western societies? Is it culturally bound? What psychiatric disorders are culturally bound?

☐ References

American Psychiatric Association. (1994). *Diagnostic and statistical manual of mental disorders* (4th ed.). Washington, DC: Author.

☐ Suggested Readings

Arnold, S. E. (1999). Cognition and neuropathology in schizophrenia. *Acta Psychiatrica Scandinavica Supplementum, 395,* 41–50.

Canuso, C. M., Goldstein, J. M., & Green, A. I. (1998). The evaluation of women with schizophrenia. *Psychopharmacological Bulletin, 34,* 271–277.

Clark, A. F., & Lewis, S. W. (1998). Treatment of schizophrenia in childhood and adolescence. *Journal of Child Psychology and Psychiatry, 39,* 1071–1081.

Coffey, M. (1998). Schizophrenia: A review of current research and thinking. *Journal of Clinical Nursing, 7,* 489–498.

Duncan, G. E., Sheitman, B. B., & Lieberman, J. A. (1999). *Brain Research, Brain Research Reviews, 29,* 250–264.

Ereshefsky, L. (1999). Pharmacologic and pharmacokinetic considerations in choosing an antipsychotic. *Journal of Clinical Psychiatry, 60,* 20–30.

Fleck, S. (1998). Impediments in the treatment of schizophrenic patients. *Connecticut Medicine, 62,* 707–714.

Glenthoj, B. Y., & Hemmingsen, R. (1999). Transmitter dysfunction during the process of schizophrenia. *Acta Psychiatrica Scandinavica Supplementum, 395,* 105–112.

Gur, R. E., & Chin, S. (1999). Laterality in functional brain imaging studies of schizophrenia. *Schizophrenia Bulletin, 25,* 141–156.

Kane, J. M. (1999). Management strategies for the treatment of schizophrenia. *Journal of Clinical Psychiatry, 60,* 13–17.

Knapp, M. (1997). Costs of schizophrenia. *British Journal of Psychiatry, 171,* 509–518.

Lieberman, J. A. (1999). Pathophysiologic mechanisms in the pathogenesis and clinical course of schizophrenia. *Journal of Clinical Psychiatry, 60,* 9–12.

Malla, A. K., Norman, R. M., & Voruganti, L. P. (1999). Improving outcome in schizophrenia. *Canadian Medical Association Journal (CMAJ), 160,* 843–860.

Meltzer, H. Y. (1999). Outcome in schizophrenia: Beyond symptom reduction. *Journal of Clinical Psychiatry, 60,* 3–7.

Neumann, P. J. (1999). Methods of cost-effectiveness analysis in the evaluation of new antipsychotics: Implications for schizophrenia treatment. *Journal of Clinical Psychiatry, 60,* 9–14.

Parnas, J. (1999). From predisposition to psychosis: Progression of symptoms in schizophrenia. *Acta Psychiatrica Scandinavica Supplementum, 395,* 20–29.

Ross, C. A. (1999). Schizophrenia genetics: Expansion of knowledge? *Molecular Psychiatry, 4,* 4–5.

Rund, B. R. (1998). Review of longitudinal studies of cognitive functions in schizophrenia patients. *Schizophrenia Bulletin, 24,* 425–435.

Schultz, S. K., & Andreasen, N. C. (1999). Schizophrenia. *Lancet, 353,* 1425–1430.

Tsuang, M. T., & Faraone, S. V. (1999). The concept of target features in schizophrenia research. *Acta Psychiatrica Scandinavica Supplementum, 395,* 2–11.

Willner, P. (1997). The dopamine hypothesis of schizophrenia: Current status, future prospects. *International Clinical Psychopharmacology, 12,* 297–308.

Delusional Disorder

☐ Introduction

Delusional disorder is characterized by one or several delusions or false, unshakable beliefs that are present for at least a month, that are described as nonbizarre, usually meaning that similar beliefs or ideas could be rational if they had a basis in reality in some other context. For example, that someone has stolen your soul or that some machine is putting thoughts into your head would be considered bizarre, while the idea that someone might be following you could indeed have a basis in reality, and would thus be nonbizarre.

Several subtypes of delusional disorders have been described, and the DSM-IV recognizes these, including: a) erotomanic type (the idea that some person is in love with you who really isn't); b) grandiose type (the idea that you have special gifts or talents or have made some spectacular discovery when you haven't); c) jealous type (the belief that your spouse or lover is unfaithful when there is no objective evidence for this); d) persecutory type (the belief that you are being followed, tracked, or spied upon, despite a lack of objective evidence); e) somatic type (involving bodily functions or sensation, such as, the idea that you are emitting a foul odor); and f) mixed and unspecified types.

In the following scenario please notice the following:

1) Some disorders, such as schizophrenia, result in marked social impairment from early in the course of the illness. Is that the case with delusional disorder? If not, why not?

2) Contrast this case report to that of the individual with schizophrenia. How can one differentially diagnose these two conditions? What are the major differences in presentation? Course? Outcome?

☐ Diagnostic Criteria
(DSM-IV)

A. Nonbizarre delusions (i.e., involving situations that occur in real life, such as being followed, poisoned, infected, loved at a distance, or deceived by spouse or lover, or having a disease) of at least one month's duration.
B. Criterion A for schizophrenia has never been met. **Note:** Tactile and olfactory hallucinations may be present in Delusional Disorder if they are related to the delusional theme.
C. Apart from the impact of the delusion(s) or its ramifications, functioning is not markedly impaired and behavior is not obviously odd or bizarre.
D. If mood episodes have occurred concurrently with delusions, their total duration has been brief relative to the duration of the delusional periods.
E. The disturbance is not due to the direct physiological effects of a substance (e.g., a drug of abuse, a medication) or a general medical condition.

☐ The Stories

I

Marge Norris was regarded by all of her colleagues as a very competent nurse. She had risen through the ranks at her hospital and was now the Nurse Manager on one of the Surgery ICUs. She was admired for her leadership skills, patience, ability to resolve interpersonal conflicts among her staff, and the efficiency on her unit. She took her job very seriously and saw it as her life. She had been divorced some 20 years. Her two children, now both in their mid-20s had flown the nest several years before, and both were doing quite well. Her daughter, Janice, had moved to the east coast, was married, had a job as a teacher, and was expecting her first child this summer. Her son, John, was in graduate school in Michigan, studying philosophy (I wonder how he became interested in that—certainly not from me) she thought.

She prided herself on her quiet efficiency and the care that was delivered on her unit.

In recent months, something new had entered her life. She had become aware of the fact that Dr. Connors, the new orthopedic surgeon, who was much admired by all the nurses for his dedication, hard work, late nights, and warm and caring bedside manner, seemed to be showing a special interest in her. She first became aware of his attraction to her in subtle ways. He seemed to stop by the nursing station more than was necessary, and requested her presence when making rounds on his patients. He would go out of his way to ask her advice on certain issues. She was surprised no one else had noticed his affection. She wouldn't mention it to anyone else anyway. (He probably wants it kept secret.) She was quite sure that they shared this common bond, and that it would continue to grow and develop. She was in no hurry to force it forward prematurely.

She had a hard time describing the nature of the relationship, even to herself. Was it romantic? Clearly that was part of it. She could tell by the way he looked at her that he cared a great deal about her, not just as a nurse and fellow professional, but also as a woman. Was it sexual? The fact that she was at least 15 years older than he didn't seem to bother him, why should it bother her? It certainly hadn't been overtly sexual, and she wasn't sure whether it ever would be or not, although she didn't think it necessary for it to be sexual. It was more that she and Dr. Connors shared a common vision of how medicine should be practiced. She saw them as two crusaders, caring for patients, working long hours, forsaking personal needs for the welfare of their charges. Other doctors and nurses didn't understand this bond, perhaps *couldn't* understand it.

But when Dr. Connors was tied up in the Operating Room for long hours, or out of town, she missed him greatly. She sometimes needed to reestablish contact with him. She had started calling his home occasionally. It hurt and upset her when his wife or children answered, since she knew that his love for her made it impossible for him to give his family the love they deserved as well. She knew he was the sort of man that could really love only one woman, could only really be bonded with one other person, and she was increasingly convinced that it was she. So, she pitied his wife and felt sorry for his children, but she called anyway to hear his voice, and when he said his name she would linger a moment before hanging up. She didn't want to do this too often because she thought this would arouse his concerns, but she thought perhaps now she could detect in his voice that he knew it was she who was calling, even if she said nothing.

At various times she had fantasies about confronting him with her knowledge of his feelings for her. She thought up various ways to do it and fantasized about it sitting in the nursing station. In her fantasies, when she confronted him with what she knew to be his feelings, he would embrace her; at other times shake her hand, and affirm his deep commitment to her. His exact reaction varied, but in her fantasy, this would be the turning point when they would begin sharing the rest of their lives together. Not just there in the Intensive Care Unit, but at other times as well. She fantasized about traveling with him to medical meetings, what they would do on the weekends, the serious talks they would have about all the changes in health care, new orthopedic surgery procedures, steps forward in nursing practice. One night she almost burst forward with her confrontation when the two of them were briefly alone in the nursing station. But no, the time was not appropriate and she decided afterwards that the safest way to make him aware that she knew how he felt was by giving him a note. The next day when he had made rounds and was about to leave the unit after seeing his patients, she handed him a sealed envelop marked "personal" on the outside. She took him aside briefly, and asked him to read it later when he was alone. The letter read:

Dear James,

   I'm sending you this note to let you know that I understand your feelings for me. I've known now for some time how you've felt about me and the bond that we share as doctor and nurse but also as man and woman. I admire you greatly and feel that you are a very special physician who is destined to influence lives and help many individuals. I am willing to talk with you about our future, if you are ready.

—Marge

II

Dr. James Connors sat in his office chatting with Judy Carter, Director of Nursing at the hospital. He had called Judy earlier that morning, asking to see her as soon as possible about one of her staff. Although Dr. Connors was relatively new to the facility, the nursing director knew he was well liked and highly respected, and she was concerned that he might have some complaint regarding how her staff was performing. She found Dr. Connors' air of comfort and calm reassuring.

"What's up Jim?" she began and fixed her eyes on the surgeon across the desk from her. She liked this man a great deal. He must be about the age of her own son, who was a cardiologist in Pittsburgh. Dr. Connors and her son had much in common including an ethic that dictated hard work and unconditional concern for their patients.

As usual, Dr. Connors was direct, "Judy, some funny things have been going on with Marge, the head nurse on the surgical ICU on five. I don't know exactly how to say this and I don't want to hurt the reputation of one of your best head nurses, but I think something has got to be done. The easiest way to begin is probably to have you read this note. Marge gave it to me late yesterday and asked me to read it when I was alone. Perhaps you should read it before we talk."

Dr. Connors passed the letter across the desk and settled back into his chair. He took out his laptop and started making notes to himself of things that he needed to check on that afternoon. (No reason to waste time.)

When the director of nursing had finished the note she was puzzled and alarmed. "It would appear that she thinks you have been signaling her in some way that you are interested in her. Do you spend extra time with her? Do you have any kind of special relationship with her?

Dr. Connors shook his head. "No. She's an excellent nurse and because of that at times I request her to round with me, and we are friendly to each other, but it's never seemed romantic to me in the least. I mean, she is nearly old enough to be my mother. I don't think it is anything that I am doing. If it is, let me know and I'll try to change it, but I don't think that's what is going on. I think it's in her head."

Judy asked, "Have you tried to talk this over with her?"

"No, I thought I would come and talk with you first."

"Any other notes?"

"No, only the one, although I think she has been acting somewhat odd around me, looking at me too long, hanging around me when I'm in the nursing station or out on the unit."

Judy was perplexed and concerned, "If it's all right with you I'm going to talk this over with John Bradberry. He's probably still rounding upstairs on the psychiatry service. I think I'll go up there now and see if I can catch him."

Dr. Connors said, "Well, I'll wait to hear from you and I would very much appreciate your help in this matter."

☐ Discussion

In considering these stories, notice several features. First, the head nurse's functioning for the most part is well preserved. Her delusion appears to focus on one isolated area—that she and Dr. Connors have a special bond and are somehow linked. She has also been discrete about her delusion, sharing her belief only with him. Also, the age of onset is of interest, occurring in middle age. All of these features (the relative preservation of psychosocial functioning, the isolation of the delusion, the nonbizarre nature of the delusion, and the relatively late age of onset) tend to differentiate this disorder from schizophrenia.

We have no evidence of cognitive impairment, which makes it unlikely that this is a psychotic disorder secondary to some medical condition or dementia. Also, we have no evidence that the problem is drug induced. Mood symptoms do not appear to be prominent and therefore a psychotic mood disorder appears unlikely.

Delusional disorder is a relatively rare psychotic condition in which the affected individual develops one or more nonbizarre delusions. Problems in functioning can result. For example, we have evidence here that this individual is soon to encounter some occupational problems following her decision to send a note to the person she thinks is in love with her.

This is generally a disorder that begins in middle age or late life and can often be chronic. It occurs only rarely (lifetime prevalence estimates of .05 to .1). There isn't any clear evidence that delusional disorder is familial. The treatment of this condition generally centers on the use of antipsychotic drugs with supportive, insight oriented psychotherapy. However, these patients are not highly motivated for treatment and even those who submit to treatment many times do not respond.

☐ Questions for Further Discussion

1) Think up examples of the other subtypes of delusional disorder.
2) What are other examples of bizarre delusions?
3) How do you think Marge will respond if she is confronted by Judy?
4) If Dr. Connors told her that there was no basis for her assumption, do you think she would believe him?

☐ References

American Psychiatric Association. (1994). *Diagnostic and statistical manual of mental disorders* (4th ed.). Washington, DC: Author.

☐ Further Readings

Howard, R. (1996). Drug treatment of schizophrenia and delusional disorder in late life. *International Psychogeriatrics, 8,* 597–608.

Manschreck, T. C. (1996). Delusional disorder: The recognition and management of paranoia. *Journal of Clinical Psychiatry, 57,* 32–38.

Silva, A. J., Ferrari, M. M., Leong, G. B., & Penny, G. (1998). The dangerousness of persons with delusional jealousy. *Journal of the American Academy of Psychiatry Law, 26,* 607–623.

Silva, J. A., Harry, B. E., Leong G. B., & Weinstock, R. (1996). Dangerous delusional misidentification and homicide. *Journal of Forensic Science, 41,* 641–644.

Soares, J. C., & Gershon, S. (1997). Therapeutic targets in late-life psychoses: Review of concepts and critical issues. *Schizophrenia Research, 27,* 227–239.

IV MOOD DISORDERS

Mood disorders are, as the name implies, disorders of mood or affect. There are disorders of low mood (depression) or high mood (mania), although, as usual, things are not quite that simple. Categories of mood disorder include major depressive disorder, which is classically referred to as clinical depression (which will be illustrated here), and dysthymic disorder which is generally a less severe form of depression that tends to be chronic, lasting at least 2 years. Depressive disorder not otherwise specified is the coding term for depressions that fall outside of these guidelines. Mood disorders can also be induced by medical conditions (for example, thyroid dysfunction) and by the ingestion of certain substances (drugs such as cocaine or psychostimulants). Bipolar disorder characterized by both depression and mania will also be illustrated (in the manic phase). Bipolar I includes full blown depressions and manias. Bipolar II tends to be characterized by less severe mania (so called hypomania) and depression. The term cyclothymia is applied to individuals who tend to have mood cycling but not to the same degree of severity as patients with bipolar disorder.

In most psychiatric practices and general health care settings, major depression is one of the most common disorders seen, and therefore we will begin with that disorder. Mania will be discussed in Chapter 8.

Depression

☐ Introduction

Depression is one of the most common, best described, and treatable psychiatric disorders. Depression is not just seen by mental health practitioners; it accounts for many office visits to general practitioners and other medical specialists as well. People with depression many times do not realize they are depressed. They often perceive their illness as personal failure, or, not uncommonly, as a physical problem. Therefore, unfortunately, many times individuals with depression do not receive proper treatment, despite the fact that effective treatments have been developed that benefit most patients with depression.

The stories that follow illustrate a case of major depressive disorder occurring in a nurse. We are able to see how the person affected views her problem (she doesn't see it as an illness, but as evidence of her failure), and how the man she is dating sees the problem (he sees it as a growing lack of interest on her part). In reading these stories, consider the following points:

1) At no point in either story is the word depression mentioned by the nurse or her boyfriend. Why?
2) Is there any evidence that this depression is "psychotic" (that it involves delusions or hallucinations)?
3) As you read the stories make a list of the symptoms of depression that this patient is experiencing, or that others observe.

☐ Diagnostic Criteria
(DSM-IV)

A. Five (or more) of the following symptoms have been present during the same two-week period and represent a change from previous functioning; at least one of the symptoms is either (1) depressed mood or (2) loss of interest or pleasure.
Note: Do not include symptoms that are clearly due to a general medical condition, or mood-incongruent delusions or hallucinations.

1) Depressed mood most of the day, nearly every day, as indicated by either subjective report (e.g., feels sad or empty) or observation made by others (e.g., appears tearful). **Note**: In children and adolescents, can be irritable mood.
2) Markedly diminished interest or pleasure in all, or almost all, activities most of the day, nearly every day (as indicated by either subjective account or observation made by others).
3) Significant weight loss when not dieting or weight gain (e.g., a change of more than 5% of body weight in a month), or decrease or increase in appetite nearly every day. **Note**: In children, consider failure to make expected weight gains.
4) Insomnia or hypersomnia nearly every day.
5) Psychomotor agitation or retardation nearly every day (observable by others, not merely subjective feelings of restlessness or being slowed down).
6) Fatigue or loss of energy nearly every day.
7) Feelings of worthlessness or excessive or inappropriate guilt (which may be delusional) nearly every day (not merely self-reproach or guilt about being sick)
8) Diminished ability to think or concentrate, or indecisiveness, nearly every day (either by subjective account or as a observed by others).
9) Recurrent thoughts of death (not just fear of dying), recurrent suicidal ideation without a specific plan, or a suicide attempt or a specific plan for committing suicide.

B. The symptoms do not meet criteria for a Mixed Episode.
C. The symptoms cause clinically significant distress or impairment in social, occupational, or other important areas of functioning.
D. The symptoms are not due to the direct physiological effects of a substance (e.g., a drug of abuse, a medication) or a general medical condition (e.g., hypothyroidism).
E. The symptoms are not better accounted for by Bereavement, i.e., after the loss of a loved one, the symptoms persist for longer than

two months or are characterized by marked function impairment, morbid preoccupation with worthlessness, suicidal ideation, psychotic symptoms, or psychomotor retardation.

☐ The Stories

I

John Gault had been dating Teresa Robinson for nearly a year. Although they were both 30, their lives had been very different. John was a hard driving businessman who had taken over his father's automobile dealership after finishing college and had expanded it dramatically, adding a used car lot and a new line of an overseas model. He had been a high school football player, outgoing and popular, and a good student in college. He was now a success in his business. He had never married, which was somewhat surprising given his good looks, financial resources, and social skills.

Teresa Robinson, on the other hand, had a difficult adolescence. Her father had died prematurely of heart disease when she was 12 and her mother, an elementary school teacher, had raised Teresa and her two older brothers alone. Money was tight and there never had been the extra dollars for the special things she wanted, although her mother had provided for the children as best she could. After graduating, Teresa had married her high school sweetheart, and soon became pregnant. At 21 she had her second child. There were problems with the marriage from the beginning. Her husband, always a heavy drinker, started spending nights away from home, and it became increasingly apparent that he was involved with other women. Despite her concerns about the burden of having two small children, Teresa left him, got an apartment, and sued for divorce, showing the same tenacity her mother had shown. She started college while working nights and weekends. She found she had an affinity for biological sciences, entered a nursing program, and graduated at the age of 28. Since then she had worked as an E.R. nurse, finding the work both interesting and challenging, and her kids were doing well in school. She had friends, and she had been quite content with her life and her family, until she met John while shopping for a car. Things just clicked, and they had been dating since, negotiating the various tasks of intimacy that presented themselves in a successful relationship. She found a new happiness that she had never really experienced before.

However, around Christmas, about six months ago, for some unexplained reason, things began to change. She found she couldn't get into the holiday spirit. Her children were excited, of course, and she had always enjoyed the holidays, decorating the house, and socializing with friends. But last Christmas things had been different, and things had continued that way since.

John had noticed the change and sensed that she was losing interest in him. He had become increasingly irritable and distant, which only seemed to make matters worse.

He invited her out to the restaurant where they had gone on their first date; a romantic Italian place not far from the hospital where she worked. He picked her up at seven and by 7:30 they were comfortably seated in the booth toward the back of the restaurant with an antipasto and two glasses of chianti between them. Teresa seemed as distant as John had ever seen her.

After the pleasantries, with a lump in his throat, he again began to tell her of his concerns, "Teresa, I really don't know what to say. I thought things were going so well between us. We seemed to really hit it off. Knowing you during this last year has been very important to me. Getting to know your kids has been more fun than I imagined possible and I think they really like me. But its clear that something has happened between us and I don't know what to do."

There was silence from Teresa. She was staring off into the distance, seemingly disinterested in the conversation.

"Teresa, you've got to talk to me. This is important. What are you thinking?"

"Oh, I'm sorry. I'm just distracted, something that happened at work."

"Well, please tell me about it," said John, initially irritated but shifting to a sympathetic tone.

"Janie, my supervisor, talked with me today. She's going to put a note of concern in my personnel file." She shook her head from side to side and stared at the table.

"What happened?" asked John.

"It had to do with a patient in the E.R. the night before last. A mother had brought in her son who had fallen in a gym and cut open his chin. I paged Dr. Sutherland to come and do the stitching, but he didn't pick up his page, and I totally forgot about it. The mother and child ended up sitting in the room for two hours before one of the other nurses found them there. I can't believe I forgot about them. I can't believe the things I forget now. I don't think I'm really cut out to be a nurse. I don't seem to care enough about my patients, and don't give them good care. I've even thought about leaving nursing and getting some other kind of job. People depend on me and I'm letting them down."

"Wait a minute," said John, "you love nursing and your patients have always liked you. You're good at what you do. Everyone thinks so."

"Not anymore," replied Teresa. "I feel like I'm in a fog all the time. It's like I'm in a cloud. Part of it is that I don't sleep very well."

"That I wouldn't know. It's been weeks since you've asked me to stay over. It's clear you're not interested in being intimate with me anymore."

"I'm sorry. I know I've let you down as well, but I can't sleep. I lay awake at night thinking about things I've done and things I've said, and people I've hurt."

John was genuinely concerned. "Look, I wonder if you're sick. You've clearly lost weight. You hardly eat a thing when we eat together, and you never want to go anywhere. We used to get together with Fred and Alice all the time. I can't remember the last time we went out. You used to love to go to movies but we haven't been to a movie since before Christmas. You used to love Italian food but you haven't even touched the antipasto."

Teresa continued to stare at the table, slowly shaking her head from side to side. Then John became insistent. "Terri, you have to talk to me. I have to know what's wrong. I want to know if you're sick. I think you need to see a doctor."

Tears came into Teresa's eyes and she began to cry. John reached across the table and touched her shoulder and thought to himself (Good. It's good for people to cry.)

When she had sobbed for a minute or so he began to ask as gently and supportively as he could, "Please tell me what's wrong."

She said in a hushed voice, "I'm so very sorry. I've let you down, I've let my patients down, I've let my children down, and I've let God down. Everything is ruined and there is nothing anyone can do about it."

II

Teresa Robinson left work at the emergency room. (Thank God it was a slow night, I couldn't have handled it otherwise.) and drove her Buick station wagon home. She felt tired. So very tired (What happened to my energy? I used to have so much and now it's all gone.).

She arrived home around midnight. The children were asleep. There was a message from her boyfriend on the answering machine telling her to call regardless of how late she got in, but she wasn't in the mood for conversation. She also wasn't hungry, and never even turned on the kitchen light. Instead, she went into the living room and sat on the couch in the dark, the only light coming from the entrance hall and the faint lights from the houses across the street through the front window. This was her usual routine. (No reason to try to sleep.) since she knew she would only toss and turn for two or three hours (They say if you can't sleep it's better to get up, so why even go to bed yet.). Her thoughts wandered. (Let's review how I did tonight. I have to watch myself. I'm always forgetting things. I did okay with that boy's family but I was short with the man who was having the GI bleed. I wasn't kind to him the way a nurse should be. I was short and intolerant and not nice. I used to think I was a good nurse, but no longer. I seem to have forgotten all the things I knew. I have lost my ability to work with people. I don't know what's wrong with me. I don't know why I keep screwing up. I really am sort of a worthless person. I wonder if the children would be better off without me? Perhaps a better person would raise them. Perhaps they would be happier. They are going to turn out badly this way, having me for their mother. I'm not the mother they need. I'm so tired of being anxious and nervous all the time.) She was then aware that she had been crying for several minutes.

(I'm so tired of this. I wish I could just go to sleep and sleep forever.) Teresa had recently started having fantasies of killing herself. She knew how she would do it. She had access at the hospital to plenty of medications that would kill her. She would simply make sure that her children were on sleepovers, take the necessary medication home with her, perhaps leave a note, perhaps not, take the pills, go to bed, fall asleep, and forget everything. She hadn't figured out though how she would prevent the kids from finding her. Sometimes she played with alternative strategies; for example, going to a motel so that someone else would find her.

Teresa had always been a religious person. She didn't always go to church but prayer had always been part of her life. In the last few months she found herself praying several times a day for relief, for forgiveness. She had come to believe that she must have displeased God in some way. Maybe it was the fact that she no longer was a good nurse. She had always seen her work as a nurse as part of Christian charity but now of course she had failed. She failed every day, and perhaps God wanted her to suffer for that. Perhaps she was being punished by God.

☐ Discussion

Major depressive disorder is classified as either a single episode or recurrent if two or more episodes occur. Relative to satisfying criteria, we have evidence that this individual has been depressed for about six months, since before Christmas. We don't know for sure if she's depressed every day, but clearly the story implies that that is probably the case. We know that she has lost interest in things (e.g., movies). We're not informed about any actual change in weight although we do know that her appetite is decreased and that she looks thinner. She suffers from insomnia. Psychomotor activity is not adequately presented, but she has experienced a loss of energy, has had feelings of worthlessness, appears to have difficulty concentrating, and has recurrent thoughts of death, including a specific suicide plan. She has both significant distress and impairment in her occupational and social functioning. We have no evidence that the disorder is due to a medical condition or misuse of a drug. There is no history to suggest that this might be bereavement. In short, this is a fairly classical, straightforward case of major depression. What is illustrated in this scenario, and also commonly encountered in patients with depression, is a lack of appreciation for the fact that they are suffering from depression. Rather than thinking, "I am depressed," they believe they have failed, have let people down, and that they are making mistakes. Hence, many people with depression do not seek treatment. It is important to notice that the identified patient in this case is a nurse, a person one would assume would be fairly knowledgeable about this condition, but again her insight into the problem she is having is quite limited. It is also of note that her boyfriend, who seems to be a perceptive individual, initially thinks that her symptoms represent a lack of interest in him rather than something endogenous with the patient.

Major depressive disorder is surprisingly and unfortunately a common condition among adults, with a lifetime prevalence rate of 10–25% in women and 5–10% in men. This disorder may begin at any age, but frequently begins in the 20s. A subgroup of individuals with major depression have psychotic features in that they are delusional or hallucinate. This individual appears to have developed the possible delusion that her current problems represent a punishment by God.

Major depression is associated with a variety of other forms of psychopathology and typically occurs as a comorbid condition with eating disorders, anxiety disorders, and substance use disorders. Although neglected for a long of time, major depressive disorder is now recognized as a not-uncommon phenomenon in children and adolescents as well.

The differential diagnoses one must consider are substance-induced or medically-induced problems (which do not appear to be present here although we need additional data in this regard), bipolar disorder (we have no history of mania), and dementia (although we have evidence of memory impairment, it is not of a degree where one would be highly suspect of dementia).

The course of this disorder is highly variable. Most patients develop a recurrent pattern and the prior pattern tends to predict the future pattern: people who frequently have episodes are more likely to continue to have frequent episodes later in life. Major depressive disorder is much more common in the first degree relatives of those who are affected, suggesting a substantial heritability for this condition.

Complications of this disorder, in addition to social and occupational impairment include a markedly increased risk of suicide. As many as 10–15% of patients with major depressive disorder end up dying by suicide in some studies. Substance abuse also is commonly seen, as many people attempt to medicate themselves with alcohol or drugs.

Of note, the period following childbirth appears to be a high risk period for the development of major depressive disorder (e.g., post-partum depression in women).

Although there are no specific laboratory parameters that can be monitored in making the diagnosis of major depressive disorder, underlying physiological abnormalities are commonly associated with the disorder, including dysregulation in the hypothalmo-pituitary adrenal axis (a hormonal regulatory system) and changes in sleep architecture (the stages of change in brain electrical activity that people traverse during sleep).

A number of effective treatments have been developed for major depressive disorder, and are now widely employed in clinical practice. One treatment that is commonly employed is medication. Several classes of medications are currently available. The older drugs, referred to as tricyclics because of their chemical structure, and the monoamine oxidase inhibitors (MAOIs) which suppress an enzyme involved in breaking down certain neurotransmitters, are not widely used now because of their side effects. More recently, a variety of non-tricyclic agents, sometimes referred to as the heterocyclics, have come on the market, as have five drugs that specifically target serotonin (so called serotonin reuptake inhibitors). These drugs have become the most commonly used treatments for depression.

Certain forms of psychotherapy have also been shown to be highly effective for adult major depressive patients who are not psychotic. The two that have been studied most intensively are cognitive behavioral therapy and interpersonal therapy, both highly structured manual-based approaches that have been shown in empirical trials to be quite effective with this group of patients. Also, electroconvulsive therapy (shock therapy) is an effective treatment for depression although it is not commonly used because of the medical issues involved (the need for general anesthesia) and the social stigma attached to its usage.

☐ Questions for Further Discussion

1) In most studies, a sizeable subgroup of patients who present to general physicians with physical complaints have an underlying depression. How could one screen for depression and identify these patients?
2) Do you think that depression may represent a moral weakness or lack of character?
3) What would you do if you had a friend or family member who started evidencing symptoms of depression? How could you intervene? What would you suggest to them?
4) Why do you think depression is more common in women than men?

☐ References

American Psychiatric Association. (1994). *Diagnostic and statistical manual of mental disorders* (4th ed.). Washington, DC: Author.

☐ Suggested Readings

Angst, J. (1999). Major depression in 1998: Are we providing optimal therapy? *Journal of Clinical Psychiatry, 60,* 509.

Bakish, D. (1999). The patient with comorbid depression and anxiety: The unmet need. *Journal of Clinical Psychiatry, 60,* 20–24.

Blehar, M. C., & Oren, D. A. (1997). Gender differences in depression. *Medscape Women's Health, 2,* 3.

Bottomley, A. (1998). Depression in cancer patients: A literature review. *European Journal of Cancer Care (Engl), 7,* 181–191.

Davidson, J. R., & Meltzer-Brody, S. E. (1999).The under-recognition and under-treatment of depression: What is the breadth and depth of the problem? *Journal of Clinical Psychiatry, 60,* 4–11.

Epperson, C. N. (1999). Postpartum major depression: Detection and treatment. *American Family Physician, 59,* 2247–2260.

Evans, D. L., Staab, J. P., Petitto, J. M., Morrison, M. F., Szuba, M. P., Ward, H. E., Wingate, B., Luber, M. P., & O'Reardon, J. P. (1999). Depression in the medical setting: Biopsychological interactions and treatment considerations. *Journal of Clinical Psychiatry, 60,* 40–55.

Gliatto, M. F., & Rai, A. K. (1999). Evaluation and treatment of patients with suicidal ideation. *American Family Physician, 59,* 1500–1506.

Harrington, R., Whittaker, J., & Shoebridge, P. (1998). Psychological treatment of depression in children and adolescents. A review of treatment research. *British Journal of Psychiatry, 173*, 291–298.

Kishimoto, H., Yamada, K., Iseki, E., Kosaka, K., & Okashi, T. (1998). Brain imaging of affective disorders and schizophrenia. *Psychiatry and Clinical Neuroscience, 52*, S212–S214.

Magruder, K. M., & Norquist, G. S. (1999). Structural issues and policy in the primary care management of depression. *Journal of Clinical Psychiatry, 60*, 29425–30742.

Schade, C. P., Jones, E. R. Jr., & Wittlin, B. J. (1998). A ten-year review of the validity and clinical utility of depression screening. *Psychiatric Services, 49*, 55–61.

Schulberg, H. C., Katon, W. J., Simon, G. E., & Rush, A. J. (1999). Best clinical practice: Guidelines for managing major depression in primary medical care. *Journal of Clinical Psychiatry, 60*, 19–28.

Scott, J., Gilvarry, E., & Farrell, M. (1998). Managing anxiety and depression in alcohol and drug dependence. *Addictive Behavior, 23*, 919–931.

Small, G. W. (1998). Treatment of geriatric depression. *Depression and Anxiety, 1*, 32–42.

Souery, D., Amsterdam, J., de Montigny, C., Lecrubier, Y., Montgomery, S., Lipp, O., Racagni, G., Zohar, J., & Mendlewicz, J. (1999). Treatment resistant depression: Methodological overview and operational criteria. *European Journal of Neuropsychopharmacology, 9*, 83–91.

Starkstein, S. E., & Robinson, R. G. (1996). Mood disorders in neurodegenerative diseases. *Seminars in Clinical Neuropsychiatry, 1*, 272–281.

Sutor B., Rummans T. A., Jowsey, S. G., Krahn, L. E., Martin, M. J., O'Connor, M. K., Philbrick, K. L., & Richardson, J. W. (1998). Major depression in medically ill patients. *Mayo Clinic Proceedings, 73*, 329–337.

Wulsin, L. R., Vaillant, G. E., & Wells, V. E. (1999). A systematic review of the mortality of depression. *Psychsomatic Medicine, 61*, 6–17.

CHAPTER

Mania

☐ Introduction

The vignettes that follow portray a man in the midst of a manic episode. Mania is a condition that, although episodic, can have devastating consequences for the affected individual and his or her family. In reading through the material that follows, keep in mind several points:

1) Pay attention to the onset and duration of symptoms. Is this a disorder that started a long time ago and has gotten worse recently, or is this a disorder that appears to have a fairly recent, abrupt onset? This is important in differentiating chronic psychotic illnesses such as schizophrenia from episodic psychotic illnesses such as mania.

2) Focus on the information provided regarding how quickly this individual thinks, talks, and moves, and with the rapidity that he changes from one topic to another. As you will see, everything seems speeded up.

3) Pay attention to this individual's self-control (or lack of it) and to his inability to pursue pleasurable activities in an appropriate manner. For example, most people who drink do so moderately and don't lose control. Most of us enjoy buying things and at times collecting things, but are able to exert control to an extent that we don't spend money foolishly. As we will see, this individual seems to lose control in many areas.

☐ Diagnostic Criteria
(DSM-IV)

A. A distinct period of abnormally and persistently elevated, expansive, or irritable mood, lasting at least one week (or any duration if hospitalization is necessary).
B. During the period of mood disturbance, three (or more) of the following symptoms have persisted (four if the mood is only irritable) and have been present to a significant degree:
   1) inflated self-esteem or grandiosity
   2) decreased need for sleep (e.g., feels rested after only three hours of sleep)
   3) more talkative than usual or pressure to keep talking
   4) flight of ideas or subjective experience that thoughts are racing
   5) distractibility (i.e., attention too easily drawn to unimportant or irrelevant external stimuli)
   6) increase in goal-directed activity (either socially, at work or school, or sexually) or psychomotor agitation
   7) excessive involvement in pleasurable activities that have a high potential for painful consequences (e.g., engaging in unrestrained buying sprees, sexual indiscretions, or foolish business investments)
C. The symptoms do not meet criteria for a Mixed Episode
D. The mood disturbance is sufficiently severe to cause marked impairment in occupational functioning or in usual social activities or relationships with others, or to necessitate hospitalization to prevent harm to self or others, or there are psychotic features.
E. The symptoms are not due to the direct physiological effects of a substance (e.g., a drug of abuse, a medication, or other treatment) or a general medical condition (e.g., hyperthyroidism).
   Note: Manic-like episodes that are clearly caused by somatic antidepressant treatment (e.g., medication, electroconvulsive therapy, light therapy) should not count toward a diagnosis of Bipolar I Disorder.

☐ The Stories

I

John Meyers and Larry Borden, friends for several years at a brokerage firm in Atlanta, would be attending a meeting in New York for the firm. When they had discussed the trip a week before, they were both looking forward to the opportunity of having a few nights on the town in the Big Apple. The two had had lunch together to plan the trip.

John had been somewhat concerned about Larry in the last few weeks. Steve Winthrop, a mutual friend who often played racquetball with Larry had called John a few days before the lunch to express his concern about Larry, "Man, Larry was really freaking out today. We met for our racquetball game. Larry was all over the place. He was almost bouncing off the walls more than the ball. When we first started playing I wondered if he was drunk, but I don't think so. He just really seemed hyper and got really pissed when someone else came to claim the court when our hour was up. See what you think when you have lunch with him."

John had similar concerns after the lunch, which he did not find at all reassuring. First, Larry was a half hour late. He came into the restaurant almost running. During the 45 minutes they had for lunch Larry had three vodka martinis, although he usually didn't drink during the day.

John said, "Wow Larry. You're really putting them away today. Is everything okay?"

Larry responded, "Everything is just fine. I just felt like putting some alcohol into the old system. Things just couldn't be better."

They talked about New York. Larry at one point talked about liking "New York women," an odd comment given that both were happily married, and extramarital activities had never been a part of trips to New York. John also noticed that Larry seemed to be anxious, frequently tapping his foot and at times rocking back and forth in his chair. At one point he picked up his knife and gently beat on the table like a drum. He also referred to their waitress as "babe" in ordering his third drink, which seemed clearly inappropriate to John.

Larry mentioned that he wanted to go to some art galleries on the upper east side when he was in New York. He had collected a modest amount of art through the years, mainly watercolors and drawings. Larry said he felt that he would be able to find something extremely nice for his collection. John offered to accompany him to the galleries and again asked if Larry was okay, if anything had gone wrong. Larry said everything was great.

John shared his concern with his wife that night when he got home, and anticipated the trip to New York with much trepidation. The next day he stopped by Larry's office to pick him up and share a cab to the airport. Larry was on the phone in his office so John spent the time chatting with Sarah, the secretary who sat outside Larry's glass cubicle.

Sarah had known John for several years and John knew how important Sarah's work was to Larry. Therefore, he wasn't surprised when Sarah expressed concerns as well.

"John, I'm really worried about Larry. For the last couple of weeks he's been acting really odd. He's so hyper. He never seems to settle down. He has come in late to work several times, and in the afternoon it seems to me that he has been drinking at lunch. I've never seen him do that before. He talks about all kinds of things. He started telling jokes, something he never did before, and not very funny jokes. I think you'd have to call them dirty jokes. He doesn't return phone calls, and he's been telling me he's going to make a big score in New York. He has some plan to buy art there and resell it here for a huge profit. I know he's always enjoyed art but he's never talked about it as a way of getting rich. I don't know what to do."

John took all this in, trying to put the pieces together in his mind, wondering what was happening.

(Maybe Larry's marriage is going badly.) But Larry had never mentioned anything about that and when he had last seen Larry and Jan together they seemed like their usual selves. Also, until recently, his job was going well. He was a well respected member of the firm and doing well financially. (Could he be using drugs? He seems so hyper and "speedy." Maybe this is what speed does to people.)

John said, "I don't know what's going on but I've been worried about him, too. I'll try to talk with him on the trip. Maybe he's upset about something. Maybe he needs help. I don't know, but I'll talk to him."

Sarah said, "You know, I thought about calling his wife. I'm that worried about him."

"Well, let's see how it goes in New York," said John, "We can talk more about it when I get back."

He was cut short by Larry who darted out of his office, a grin on his face, and slapped John on the back. "New York bound, John! New York bound!" said Larry emphatically.

Before John could reply Larry was behind his secretary's desk. He stood behind Sarah and placed his hands on her shoulders and began moving his hands as if he were giving her a massage.

"Sarah, you're so tense. Let me help you."

"I'm fine Larry, really," said Sarah, clearly uncomfortable with Larry's behavior.

John attempted to intervene, "Look Larry, we need to get to the airport. Let's grab a cab."

"Right you are, buddy," said Larry as he darted into his office, grabbed his wardrobe bag and headed down the hall.

The ride to the airport only heightened John's concerns. Larry talked non-stop. What he had read in the paper, what he had heard on the radio, the e-mail he had received the night before, all kinds of things. He seemed to finish one thought and then dart on to another. John tried at several points to break in, unsuccessfully.

"Larry, you're talking so fast. I'm having trouble following you," said John.

"You complain about everything, John," snapped Larry. "I hope you're not going to be a pain in the ass on this trip."

John was confused. Why would Larry talk to him like this? They had always been close and mutually supportive and now Larry seemed to have a really short fuse, which was not like him.

At the airport terminal, Larry bounded out of the cab and into the terminal, not waiting for John to catch up. The two took their place in line to check in for seat assignments. Larry seemed very impatient and said loudly enough for the people behind the ticket counter to hear, "Jesus Christ, why are they making us wait so long? This really pisses me off."

John was embarrassed. The situation worsened when Larry got to the ticket agent. It appeared that the flight was fairly full and the only seats were in the middle of the row. John couldn't believe how enraged Larry seemed. His face was red, he was clenching his teeth, demanding an aisle seat, saying that he had been a loyal customer of the airlines and didn't like being treated this way. The airline agent clearly was threatened by him and told him how she didn't like being treated this way and wouldn't tolerate his behavior. This only seemed to escalate things. Larry, again slapping the counter, demanded to see her boss. An older woman, who was evidently her supervisor, drifted down the line of agents and stood in front of Larry.

"Sir, you're going to have to calm down. You're frightening the personnel and the other passengers. If you can't control yourself, I'll have to call security."

II

Larry felt like he needed to win this racquetball game with John. John and he had been friends for years, but John could be a pain in the ass and a wimp. He was going to kick his butt on the racquetball court, or die trying (Man, am I feeling powerful and strong; why is he taking so long to serve? He is so slow.). "Hey John, your feet glued to the floor? Hubba, hubba, hubba." (John could be such a pain in the ass.)

When there was a knock on the door of the court, he yelled, "Forget it!" and turned back to face the front wall.

John said, "I'm afraid our time is up, buddy. Let's hit the shower."

Larry barked a brief, "Oh shit" as the knock on the door was heard again. He walked briskly to the door of the court, flung it open, and said emphatically with a sneer on his face, "Where's the fire?"

When Larry got back to the office he picked up his copy of Art News magazine and reviewed the plan in his mind. (I'll start hitting the dealers as soon as I get to New York. Screw the meeting. I'm going to be a hard bargainer. Then when I've bought these paintings, I'll bring them back here to Atlanta and make a fortune selling them to the galleries here.)

He had withdrawn the family savings from the bank, including a money market account totaling $10,000. He was having his stock-broker liquidate some of his other assets. He was planning on hitting the Big Apple with at least $30,000 in his pocket. He wouldn't spend that much, of course, but he found it reassuring to have that much with him in case he got lucky and found something really amazing. (My wife is such a pain in the ass. If he told her about this she would have been bloody hell to live with, although she will be more than happy to spend the money after I come back.) He was tired of Atlanta. He was looking forward to action in the big city. (I'm horny as a hootowl and if I don't get laid my first 24 hours in New York there'll be hell to pay.) He then thought about his job as a stockbroker. He wasn't really appreciated at his firm. He was clearly the smartest guy there—clearly the smartest stockbroker in Atlanta. He wondered briefly if he might not be the smartest stockbroker in the United States. (They should give an award for it.) He briefly entertained a fantasy of a convention center filled with thousands of people madly applauding as he was handed a large trophy in front of the admiring mass of people. This briefly gave way to a fantasy of picking up two attractive women in mid-town Manhattan and taking them to the Plaza Hotel.

He had lunch with John at a little Italian restaurant down the street from their brokerage firm. (John is such a pain in the ass. He's such a tight ass. He never will have a drink with me. Drinking is good for you. It settles you down, it opens you up, it gives you new ideas.) As he ordered his third vodka martini he noticed the waitress. (God our waitress looks good in that short black skirt with those black net stockings. God she looks good.) He could tell she was interested in him by the way she looked at him, the way she smiled. She wanted him. (Boy I just ought to take her into the back room right now and give her what she wants.) (Nah. You can't satisfy them all.) He chuckled to himself.

The day of the trip arrived. He was really looking forward to the Big

Apple and his score. He had been getting an amazing amount of things done. It didn't seem as if he needed nearly as much sleep anymore. If he was tired, he would sleep for a few minutes, and then be up and ready to go. Last night he'd been up half the night rearranging the books in the living room and writing down ideas for other money making schemes.

He snapped back to reality. A quick glance at the clock indicated it was time for the trip to the airport. God he felt good. As he left his office he noticed John talking with Sarah, his secretary. He had always thought that Sarah was a little plain but attractive, but in the last couple of weeks she had taken on a special meaning to him. He had come to realize that she was in love with him and wanted him. Recently he had come to realize her striking attractiveness and her sexiness. She, of course, felt the same way about him, he realized, and wanted him. She had probably wanted him for years. He'd never thought about it, but now he realized it was true and he thought maybe he would get around to her when he got back from New York. (If I have anything left.) He chuckled to himself.

He circled around behind Sarah's desk and began firmly to massage her shoulders, knowing she wanted him too, although she was probably embarrassed by John being there. "Sarah, you're so tense. Let me help you," he said.

"I'm fine Larry, really," said Sarah. (She loves every minute of this, but is embarrassed that John is here. I know she wants to turn around and take me in her arms.)

Later at the airport Larry became very frustrated waiting in line. (Why are these people so slow? Why can't they show us some respect?) He quickly looked up and down the various lines, trying to find one in which he could be served more quickly, but decided he would be equally frustrated in any line. Then he caught the ticket salesperson's eye. She was looking at him. She was looking at him and then she looked at another of the other ticket agents, who was looking at her. They knew he was there. (They are purposely slowing down ticket sales to frustrate me. All of the ticket sellers are involved. Yeah, they are probably all involved. It probably has something to do with my plans to make big money on art. They know about it and they don't want me to get to New York so they can go instead. So they can steal my plan, take my money.) He glanced up and down the ticket counter. (Yes, it's clear now, they are all involved.) He decided to fight back, "Jesus Christ, why are they making us wait so long? This really pisses me off," he said to John loudly enough for most of the passengers standing in line as well as the airline agents to hear.

The line started to move forward, but Larry had figured it out. He knew now what they were up to, but they couldn't stop him. He would show them his forcefulness and his control. He would show them who was in charge.

As he got to the ticket desk he slapped his hand firmly on the counter and said loudly in a demanding voice, "Exit row seat on the aisle. One for me and one for my friend opposite from each other." He stared menacingly at the ticket agent. (She's trying to intimidate me. She's trying to ignore me.)

Looking up worriedly from her computer screen the ticket agent said, "I'm sorry sir, all the aisle seats are taken and all the exit rows are filled. I'm afraid all I can offer you is a mid-row seat."

It all came together then for Larry. They were going to intimidate him and force him to be subservient to them and then heaven knows what they might do. Put him away somewhere so somebody else can make the money? It was clearly a plot. They were all looking at each other and looking at him. Some of the people in line were probably involved too. He found his anger boiling over, pounding the desk, yelling that he wouldn't be intimidated, that he knew what their plan was and it wouldn't work.

A woman supervisor approached him and said, "Sir, you're going to have to calm down. You're frightening the airline staff and the other passengers. If you can't control yourself, I'll have to call security."

(That's their plan. Call security and take me away and maybe kill me).

He yelled, "I know what you're up to. I know what you're trying to do and it won't work. Fuck you all," and began to swing his briefcase around him to make sure no one came near him. There was little risk of this, as the other passengers in line had quickly begun to move away from him as he escalated. At that point, two security officers were approaching from their office, and were about 10 feet away. One was armed and had his hand on his pistol handle, which was still holstered. "Sir, you're causing quite a ruckus here. I'm afraid you'll have to come with us."

(They're going to shoot me. They're going to take me someplace in the basement and shoot me. Oh my God! They're trying to kill me.) He lunged toward the officers in an effort to protect himself.

☐ Discussion

This individual presents with symptoms highly suggestive of a manic episode. In considering the DSM-IV criteria for mania, the criteria set is clearly satisfied. First, the individual has a distinct period of mood lasting a few weeks that could be characterized as evidencing, at various times, elevated, expansive, or irritable mood, therefore illustrating all three types of mood disturbance. Second, this individual does appear to have an inflated self-esteem, and at times grandiosity (regarding himself as the smartest stockbroker in Atlanta, if not in the United States), a decreased need for sleep, pressure in speech, and thoughts that are coming very rapidly (flight of ideas). He evidences an increase in goal-directed activities, and excessive involvement in pleasurable activities that have a high potential for painful consequences (liquidating assets for what appears to be inappropriate reasons, anticipating what would be considered foolish business activities that he has hidden from his wife, drinking excessively).

The individual also has evidence of impairment in relationships (misleading his wife; his friend and secretary are both very worried about him), and shows evidence of psychotic features (paranoid delusions which come to the fore in the episode at the airport at the end of the vignette). Lastly, we have no evidence that the problems are induced by substance abuse or a medical condition. Given the data we have, it would appear that this individual may be currently abusing alcohol but not drugs that are generally associated with the onset of manic-like symptoms (e.g., amphetamines, cocaine).

We need to consider medications or drugs of abuse, or concurrent medical illnesses such as hyperthyroidism (over functioning of the thyroid gland) in the differential. The list of medications, drugs of abuse, and medical conditions that can cause manic-like symptoms is quite long and for this reason patients suspected of having mania should have a careful medication history, medical history, and physical examination, and appropriate laboratory screening done as well.

Because of the presence of delusions (the suspiciousness regarding the plot against him in the airport) it is important to rule out other common causes for psychotic illness. First, although paranoid delusions would be compatible with the diagnosis of psychosis occurring in the context of a depressive illness, the mood disturbance is clearly not depressive but manic, and therefore this diagnosis can be excluded. Another illness in which delusions are commonly seen is schizophrenia. However, a diagnosis of schizophrenia requires the presence of at least two characteristic symptoms for a one month period. As mentioned, delusions are present but hallucinations, disorganize speech, grossly disorganized or catatonic behavior, and prominent negative symptoms do not appear to be present. Also, this individual shows no evidence of having had a disturbance for at least six months, which is also required for the diagnosis of schizophrenia. Therefore, there is a high probability that this individual indeed has mania.

Mania usually occurs as part of manic depressive illness, a disorder characterized by episodic mood disturbance where the affected individual is in a manic or depressive state. A subgroup of patients also go through mixed states where there appears to be a mixture of both mania and depression, a state that on first examination may seem paradoxical but which in reality occurs not uncommonly. Manic depressive illness tends to begin in adolescence or young adulthood. It is very rare to see the onset of this disorder beyond age 40. The lifetime prevalence is slightly less than 1%, and the male/female ratio is approximately equal. Manic depressive illness has a high heritability, tending to run in families. Therefore, the family history can be very helpful in making the diagnosis.

Untreated, manias generally last one to three months while untreated depressions last from two to six months or longer. Most individuals in a manic phase have poor insight into their condition and instead believe they have special gifts or abilities, or that they are being persecuted in some way.

Individuals with manic depressive illness frequently suffer significant social and occupational dysfunction because of their illness. The decisions they make when manic or depressed many times will have adverse consequences for their functioning, and it is obvious to see from our case example why such individuals would have difficulty holding jobs and maintaining relationships, given their thinking and behavior. Manic depressive illness is one of the psychiatric disorders with a markedly increased risk of suicide. Again, as illustrated by our report, excessive drinking occurs not uncommonly, particularly during the manic phase when individuals consume alcohol as a way of attempting to slow down or get sleep because of the attendant insomnia.

Knowledge about the treatment of manic depressive illness has grown steadily over the last 20 years. Now there are a number of treatment options to help these individuals through individual illness episodes, and also to help prevent future episodes. The treatment of mania, the treatment of depression, and the prophylaxis of these mood swings are three separate areas of concern. First, the traditional anti-manic drug has been lithium carbonate, which is initiated when these patients are first seen in the hospital or in the clinic. The time of onset of response to lithium is usually at minimum several days to several weeks and for that reason it was frequently prescribed in combination with antipsychotic drugs or anxiolytic drugs such as benzodiazepines to calm the patient and allow them to sleep early in treatment. The antipsychotics in particular are used for patients who are markedly agitated, intrusive, belligerent, and threatening. More recently two drugs originally used for certain forms of epilepsy, carbamazepine and valproate, have been shown to have anti-manic effects. The latter now has been FDA approved for the treatment of mania and although it is not without side effects, valproate has become the treatment of choice for many of these patients. It appears to have a somewhat earlier onset than lithium carbonate, and in general is better tolerated.

Relative to prophylaxis, the literature suggests that all three of the medications used for the treatment of mania (lithium, carbamazepine, and valproate) have prophylactic effects as well, and in particular are potent for preventing subsequent manic episodes, while they are less potent in preventing depression.

☐ Questions for Further Discussion

1) We indicated that this individual had paranoid delusions, particularly manifested at the airport at the end of the vignettes. What do we mean by paranoid, and what do we mean by delusions? Please define these terms.
2) Manic depressive illness has been linked to heightened creativity in some individuals. An interesting literature attests to the fact that a number of very creative people have had manic depressive illness. Why do you think that some people with manic depressive illness tend to be very creative?
3) What is a hallucination? If this individual were having hallucinations would the diagnosis instead be schizophrenia?

☐ References

American Psychiatric Association. (1994). *Diagnostic and statistical manual of mental disorders* (4th ed). Washington, DC: Author.

☐ Suggested Readings

Alda, M. (1997). Bipolar disorder: From families to genes. *Canadian Journal of Psychiatry*, 42, 378–387.

Berrettini, W. (1998). Progress and pitfalls: Bipolar molecular linkage studies. *Journal of Affective Disorders*, 50, 287–297.

Bland, R. C. (1997). Epidemiology of affective disorders: A review. *Canadian Journal of Psychiatry*, 42, 367–377.

Chen, S. T., Altshuler, L. L., & Spar, J. E. (1998). Bipolar disorder in late life: A review. *Journal of Geriatric Psychiatry and Neurology*, 11, 29–35.

Hilty, D. M., Brady, K. T., & Hales, R. E. (1999). A review of bipolar disorder among adults. *Psychiatric Services*, 50, 201–213.

Jope, R. S. (1999). Anti-bipolar therapy: Mechanism of actin of lithium. *Molecular Psychiatry, 4,* 117–128.

Keck, P. E., Jr., McElroy, S. I., & Strakowski, S. M. (1998). Anticonvulsants and antipsychotics in the treatment of bipolar disorder. *Journal of Clinical Psychiatry, 59,* 74–32.

Kowatch, R. A., & Bucci, J. P. (1998). Mood stabilizers and anticonvulsants. *Pediatric Clinics of North America, 45,* 1173–1186.

Licht, R. W. (1998). Drug treatment of mania: A critical review. *Acta Psychiatric Scandinavica, 97,* 387–397.

Partonen, T., & Lonnqvist, J. (1998). Seasonal affective disorder. *Lancet, 352,* 1369–1374.

Potter, W. Z. (1998). Bipolar depression: Specific treatments. *Journal of Clinical Psychiatry, 59,* 30–36.

Schatzberg, A. F. (1998). Bipolar disorder: Recent issues in diagnosis and classification. *Journal of Clinical Psychiatry, 59,* 5–12.

Scott, J. (1995). Psychotherapy for bipolar disorder. *British Journal of Psychiatry, 167,* 581–588.

Shulman, K. I., & Herrmann, N. (1999). Bipolar disorder in old age. *Canadian Family Physician, 45,* 1229–1237.

Simpson, S. G., & Jamison, K. R. (1999). The risk of suicide in patients with bipolar disorders. *Journal of Clinical Psychiatry, 60,* 53–56.

Solomon, D. A., Keitner, G. I., Ryan, C. E., & Miller, I. W. (1998). Lithium plus valproate as maintenance polypharmacy for patients with bipolar I disorder: A review. *Journal of Clinical Psychopharmacology, 18,* 38–49.

Tohen, M., & Grundy, S. (1999). Management of acute mania. *Journal of Clinical Psychiatry, 60,* 31–36.

Viguera, A. C., & Cohen, L. S. (1998). The course and management of bipolar disorder during pregnancy. *Psychopharmacology Bulletin, 34,* 339–346.

V ANXIETY DISORDERS

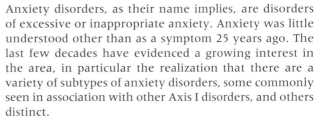

Anxiety disorders, as their name implies, are disorders of excessive or inappropriate anxiety. Anxiety was little understood other than as a symptom 25 years ago. The last few decades have evidenced a growing interest in the area, in particular the realization that there are a variety of subtypes of anxiety disorders, some commonly seen in association with other Axis I disorders, and others distinct.

Six of these disorders are illustrated here. One of the individuals suffers from panic attacks. Panic disorder can occur with our without agoraphobia (anxiety about being in certain situations in places where escape would be difficult, e.g., in a crowded room, on a bridge). Other individuals can have agoraphobia without panic attacks. Some individuals suffer from a specific phobia of a feared object or situation while others have social phobia, which involved anxiety associated with exposure to certain sorts of social situations. Also illustrated is obsessive-compulsive disorder, a fascinating condition that has been the subject of great study in the last ten years. Obsessive-compulsive disorder is characterized by obsessions or recurring intrusive thoughts and compulsions or ritualistic behaviors. Post-traumatic stress disorder (PTSD) represents the symptom residual from a traumatic event experienced earlier in life and also will be illustrated. Last to be covered will be generalized anxiety disorder, characterized by excessive fear and worry on an ongoing basis. In the DSM-IV acute distress disorder not illustrated involves symptoms similar to PTSD occurring directly after an acute stressful event. As with other categories, anxiety disorders may also be secondary to medical conditions, may be substance induced, or not otherwise specified.

Specific Phobia

☐ Introduction

This disorder, formerly referred to as simple phobia, is characterized by a significant fear of some particular thing or situation. The person realizes that this fear is excessive, overdetermined, or unreasonable. The diagnosis is made only if there is significant impairment in some area of functioning due to the fear, or if the person is markedly distressed by the symptoms.

The DSM-IV recognizes four subtypes, plus an "other" category. These include: animal phobias (e.g., insects), natural environment phobias (e.g., heights), blood/injection/injury phobias (e.g., blood drawing), and situational phobias (e.g., bridges).

In the stories that follow, examine the following questions:

1) How has this specific phobia interfered with Janet's functioning?
2) No one particularly likes to have their blood drawn, so why is Janet's fear unreasonable?
3) Notice that many of Janet's symptoms of anxiety and fear are experienced somatically. What are they?

☐ Diagnostic Criteria
(DSM-IV)

A. Marked and persistent fear that is excessive or unreasonable, cued by the presence or anticipation of a specific object or situation (e.g., flying, heights, animals, receiving an injection, seeing blood).

B. Exposure to the phobic stimulus almost invariably provokes an immediate anxiety response, which may take the form of a situationally bound or situationally predisposed Panic Attack. **Note:** In children, the anxiety may be expressed by crying, tantrums, freezing, or clinging.

C. The person recognizes that the fear is excessive or unreasonable. **Note:** In children this feature may be absent.

D. The phobic situation(s) is avoided or else is endured with intense anxiety or distress.

E. The avoidance, anxious anticipation, or distress in the feared situation(s) interferes significantly with the person's normal routine, occupational (or academic) functioning, or social activities or relationships, or there is marked distress about having the phobia.

F. In individuals under age 18 years, the duration is at least six months.

G. The anxiety, Panic Attacks, or phobic avoidance associated with the specific object or situation are not better accounted for by another mental disorder, such as Obsessive-Compulsive Disorder (e.g., fear of dirt in someone with an obsession about contamination), Post-traumatic Stress Disorder (e.g., avoidance of stimuli associated with a severe stressor), Separation Anxiety Disorder (e.g., avoidance of school), Social Phobia (e.g., avoidance of social situations because of fear of embarrassment), Panic Disorder with Agoraphobia, or Agoraphobia without History of Panic Disorder.

☐ The Stories

I

Janet Flynn, age 22, sat anxiously in the waiting area of her dentist's office. She hated being there and dreaded what would happen to her. She had a terrible fear of blood and needles, and thought that if her dentist wanted to draw blood or give her an injection, she would probably faint or pass out or scream. Sitting in the quiet waiting room she noticed that she had a visible tremor when she tried to pick up a magazine. She felt like she had butterflies in her stomach. She had a terrible sense of dread. She was afraid she was going to break down and not be able to get up and walk into the office when called.

The pain on the left side of her jaw had started about a month before. At first it was intermittent but in the last few weeks it had become constant and the last two nights she was unable to sleep because of the pain. It was unrelieved by the use of nonsteroidal anti-inflammatory drugs, and now was causing her insomnia, and this finally convinced her to call the dentist office for an emergency appointment. She had been nervous ever since and now had to restrain herself from the impulse to get up and run out of the office.

She realized this fear of blood and needles was crazy. She hadn't had it when she was a child. She remembered having her blood drawn on numerous occasions during childhood and adolescence. She also remembered being particularly sickened by the site of blood beginning in high school, when her health class had seen a film on heart surgery. She remembered the graphic depiction of the human heart with blood oozing out as the surgeon performed the operation. She had been standing at the back of the room (all the seats were taken), and became lightheaded and nauseated and had to leave the room. A few years later when she was visiting her grandmother in the hospital, she had to leave the room again when the nurse came in to draw her grandmother's blood. She felt lightheaded and dizzy, and was sure she would pass out if she stayed.

Two years before, following a pelvic exam, her family doctor said they wanted to draw a tube of blood to make sure she wasn't anemic. She immediately became panicky and was visibly shaking when she sat down in the chair in the doctor's laboratory office. She felt dizzy and faint, had a sick feeling in her stomach, and had the urge to bolt from the room. When the lab attendant inserted the needle into her left arm, everything went black and she passed out. She awakened several minutes later on the floor with a cold towel on her forehead and a pillow under her head. She hadn't seen a doctor since. She became anxious and ill now when she saw blood portrayed in a film or on television. She realized this was irrational, but she couldn't seem to control it.

She told her mother once about the problem and her mother mentioned that an aunt who always refused to go to the doctor and eventually died of cancer had had a fear of blood, and never allowed anyone to draw her blood.

She realized that she needed to have regular health care. She was told that she should have a pap smear done regularly, but she hadn't seen any health professionals in the last two years, and wouldn't have come to the dentist today if the pain wasn't unbearable.

Her boyfriend, Tom, who had accompanied her on the visit, took her hand, "Look Janet, you have to get this done. It's going to be okay. We've got to find out what is wrong. The pain is getting worse and something has to be done. I'll stay with you the whole time. Don't worry."

II

Carolyn Duke had already had a long day and was looking forward to going home in a few hours. She had to stop at the grocery on the way and pick up food for dinner, but was looking forward to a quiet evening, and to putting her feet up on the stool and relaxing and watching television. She had just finished helping the dentist cement in a crown and now stopped by the desk and picked up the file of the next patient. She proceeded down the hall to the waiting room and called out, "Janet Flynn."

Janet was shaking as she raised herself from the chair (I just can't do it. I can't do it.) She turned to Tom, "Tom, I just can't do it. My mouth is feeling better now anyway. I'm not going to stay now. I'm going to go home," and started toward the door. Tom supportively but firmly took her arm and said, "Janet, this thing is really hurting you. You have to go in and see the dentist. I'll ask them if I can come in with you and sit with you and hold your hand."

Carolyn observed all this from the doorway. She'd seen many patients who had difficulty seeing dentists or doctors. This young woman looked terrified, and Carolyn would do whatever she could to help out. She crossed the waiting room and put her hand on Janet's arm. "Janet, I'm Carolyn, one of the nurses here. Is it hard for you to come to the dentist?"

Janet was visibly shaking, "This scares me to death. I just can't stand needles and blood and things like that. It makes me pass out." Tom said, "She's afraid of needles."

Carolyn saw that she looked blanched and shaky and guided her back to the chair. Sitting down opposite her while Tom took the seat next to her, Carolyn attempted to reassure her. "Janet, I know you've been having some problems. I talked with you on the phone when you called in. Why don't we go back and let the doctor examine you. You don't have to agree to have your blood drawn or to have anything done and there will be no needles used unless you give your permission. Let the doctor just look in your mouth and see what the problem is and then we can take it from there.

Janet considered these words, breathing heavily. She seemed to visibly relax somewhat and said, "Okay. But no needles." Supported by Tom she got up and slowly walked across the room and into the dentist's office.

☐ Discussion

Relative to the diagnostic criteria, Janet's fear is excessive and unreasonable. No one likes to have their blood drawn, but most people tolerate it with minimal anxiety and don't avoid seeking health care because of it. Janet clearly has an anxiety response when just thinking about the stimulus (blood, blood drawing), and she realizes that the fear is excessive. She clearly is avoiding exposure to situations in which someone might wish to draw her blood, or in which she might be exposed to blood. Relative to the last criteria, she clearly has marked distress. Also, the fear is interfering with her obtaining the health care she needs and therefore significantly impacts on her life. We have no evidence of another type of anxiety disorder, although a careful history would be necessary before ruling out other coexisting problems.

About 10% of individuals will have a specific phobia, making this one of the most common forms of mental disorder. The age of onset varies from childhood through adulthood, although the blood/injection/injury type generally begins in childhood. Such phobias tend to be chronic and have a familial pattern.

In the differential diagnosis one must consider panic disorder with agoraphobia as well as social phobia and post-traumatic stress disorder. In obsessive-compulsive disorder, certain symptoms such as specific phobias are commonly seen, but the avoidance is associated with the content of the obsession rather than an individual stimulus. Avoidance of food in patients with eating disorders is not counted as evidence of specific phobia but instead as part of the eating disorder. Many people with the blood/injection/injury type will faint as part of their symptomatology.

The treatment of specific phobias usually involves systematic desensitization where the individual is gradually exposed to the feared object as their anxiety diminishes, or by "flooding" where the individual is exposed more aggressively to the stimulus. Both approaches have their adherents. Medications to treat anxiety, such as the benzodiazepines, are sometimes used to help people when their functioning is significantly impaired early in the course of treatment.

☐ Questions for Further Discussion

1) List other possible examples of the various subtypes of phobias.
2) Many primates are inherently afraid of snakes. How would this be possible? Is it a phobia?

☐ References

American Psychiatric Association. (1994). *Diagnostic and statistical manual of mental disorders* (4th ed.). Washington, DC: Author.

☐ **Suggested Readings**

Fyer, A. J. (1998). Current approaches to etiology and pathophysiology of specific pho-
    bia. *Biological Psychiatry*, *44*, 1295–1304.
Klein, D. F., Zitrin, C. M., Woerner, M. G., & Ross, D. C. (1983). Treatment of phobias.
    II. Behavior therapy and supportive psychotherapy: Are there any specific ingredi-
    ents? *Archives of General Psychiatry*, 40, 139–145.
Marks, M., & de Silva, P. (1994). The "match/mismatch" model of fear: Empirical status
    and clinical implications. *Behavior Research Therapy*, *32*, 759–770.
North, M. M., North, S. M., & Coble, J. R. (1998). Virtual reality therapy: An effective
    treatment for phobias. *Student Heatlh Technology Information*, *58*, 112–119.
Roth, M., & Argyle, N. (1998). Anxiety, panic, and phobic disorders: An overview.
    Journal of Psychiatric Research, *22*, 33–54.
Smalley, A. (1999). Needle phobia. *Pediatric Nursing*, *11*, 17–20.
Taylor, S. (1998). The hierarchic structure of fears. *Behavior Research and Therapy*, *36*,
    205–214.

10
CHAPTER

Panic Disorder

☐ Introduction

The essential symptom of panic disorder is the occurrence of recurrent, unexpected, and unexplainable episodes of panic that engender a great concern that the attacks will return again. The attacks must be spontaneous without evidence of any specific environmental or internal cue. Panic attacks, as described in the DSM-IV are characterized by a time-limited period of intense fear in which four or more symptoms from the following list are present:

1) palpitations, pounding heart, or accelerated heart rate
2) sweating
3) trembling or shaking
4) sensations of shortness of breath or smothering
5) feelings of choking
6) chest pain or discomfort
7) nausea or abdominal distress
8) feeling dizzy, unsteady, lightheaded, or faint
9) derealization (feelings of unreality) or depersonalization (being detached from oneself)
10) fear of losing control or going crazy
11) fear of dying
12) paresthesias (numbness or tingling sensations)
13) chills or hot flashes

In considering the following scenarios, remember the following questions:

1) Do we have evidence of agoraphobia?
2) Is there any evidence that the panic attacks are occurring in the context of some other Axis I disorder, such as major depressive disorder?
3) How can one differentiate generalized anxiety disorder from panic disorder?

☐ Diagnostic Criteria
(DSM-IV)

Panic Disorder without Agoraphobia

A. Both 1 and 2:
   1) Recurrent unexpected Panic Attacks
   2) At least one of the attacks has been followed by one month (or more) of one (or more) of the following:
      a) persistent concern about having additional attacks
      b) worry about the implications of the attack or its consequences (e.g., losing control, having a heart attack, "going crazy")
      c) a significant change in behavior related to the attacks
B. Absence of Agoraphobia
C. The Panic Attacks are not due to the direct physiological effects of a substance (e.g., a drug of abuse, a medication) or a general medical condition (e.g., hyperthyroidism).
D. The Panic Attacks are not better accounted for by another mental disorder, such as Social Phobia (e.g., occurring on exposure to feared social situations), Specific Phobia (e.g., on exposure to a specific phobic situation), Obsessive-Compulsive Disorder (e.g., on exposure to dirt in someone with an obsession about contamination), Posttraumatic Stress Disorder (e.g., in response to stimuli associated with a severe stressor), or Separation Anxiety Disorder (e.g., in response to being away from home or close relatives).

Panic Disorder with Agoraphobia

The diagnostic criteria for Panic Disorder with Agoraphobia are the same as for Panic Disorder without Agoraphobia except that Criterion

B: Absence of Agoraphobia is replaced with a new Criterion B: The Presence of Agoraphobia.

☐ The Stories

I

Danny Webb had been driving a cab for about four years, and he liked the job. The hours weren't great but it was never boring and although he would never drive a cab in a big city, driving a cab in Columbus, Ohio was just fine. It was safe, he knew the whole town by heart, and he made enough money to pay for his apartment in Germantown and buy the things he needed. He wasn't going to do it forever, and he knew it disappointed his mother, who had worked hard to go to school, and had become a high school principal at a time when few women, let alone women of African-American ancestry, got such jobs. He had always been proud of her and she of him, and he knew that eventually he would find the kind of job that would make her proud as well. For now, though, this was fine.

That had been until a few months ago, when the weirdest thing had started to happen. He had suddenly gotten very ill, but then it had gone away. He had feared he was having a heart attack, but it went away, and everything was okay. He was sure it was going to be fine, but it came back again, and now it had happened perhaps a dozen times in the last six weeks.

He had just dropped off a fare at the Ohio State campus. It was about seven in the evening, things had been quiet, and he was looking forward to turning in the cab in an hour or two and heading home. For no apparent reason, his heart started beating funny again. It felt like it was going to leap out of his chest. He could almost hear the thumping in his ears it was beating so hard. This must have been the way it was for his father when he died of a heart attack at 50. He had just dropped dead all of a sudden, and now the terrible thought came again to Danny (I'm dying of a heart attack!). He broke into a sweat and was having trouble getting his breath. He was gasping for air and he felt shaky all over, felt weak in the knees, and he found that his hands were trembling on the steering wheel. He was sure he was going to die.

He pulled the cab over to the side of the road, rolled down the window and gasped for air. He tried to take his pulse but couldn't find it. He felt like his shirt was drenched. He couldn't believe how loud his heart sounded in his chest and he felt like he was going to pass out. (Maybe I can make it to the emergency room at University Hospital. Maybe they can save my life.) He started the cab and cautiously pulled out into traffic, trembling, terrified with fear, sweating, with the constant sound of his heart beating in his ears.

II

Joyce Nolton was chatting with her colleagues in the nursing station in the emergency room when the orderly from the front desk ran in to say that there was a critical case coming in. She grabbed the crash cart, called for help, and pushed it through the metal doors. She was surprised to see a young black male, probably in his mid-20s, sitting in a chair sweating, clutching his chest, hyperventilating. She walked over to him and crouched next to the chair, placing her hand on his arm.

"Hello, I'm Joyce Nolton. What's your name?"

He gasped, "Danny Webb. Something's wrong with my heart."

It was clear to her that he was very afraid. She attempted to quickly size up the situation. He was profusely sweating, very anxious, concerned about his heart or chest, and was continuing to hyperventilate. If he continued to breathe this way he might well pass out.

"Try to stay calm Mr. Webb and we'll try to figure out what's going on."

An orderly pushed up a gurney and they helped Mr. Webb lie down on it. He was then pushed into the examining room. While Joyce took his vital signs, her colleague put in an intercath for an I.V. in the other arm and drew several tubes of blood for analysis. As soon as the I.V. was in place she handed the tubes of blood to the orderly, went into the next alcove, and got the portable EKG machine.

Joyce continued to talk to the patient, "Now Mr. Webb, tell us what happened."

"Well, I was in my cab and my heart starting beating real fast, and I think maybe I'm having a heart attack. My dad had a heart attack."

"Tell us what's going on with your heart."

"It's just beating real fast. It's beating real fast like it's going to explode." He continued to hyperventilate.

Joyce said, "Mr. Webb you're hyperventilating, which means that you're breathing too rapidly. I'd like you to try very hard to slow your breathing down. That's good. Are you having any pain in your chest?"

"Really not pain, no. It's just beating so fast and feels like it's going to explode."

Joyce asked, "Have you had any heart problems before?"

He replied, "No, not that I know of."

"Are you under the care of a doctor for any medical problems?"

"No. I see Dr. Hyman for physical exams, but everything's always been okay. Did I tell you my dad had a heart attack when he was 50?"

"Yes you did. Please tell me. Are you on any medication?" Shortly the nurses were joined by Dr. Caldwell, the E.R. physician on call. Twenty minutes later the doctor and nurses had obtained a reasonably good history, done a quick physical examination, obtained some baseline laboratory tests, vital signs, and an electrocardiogram. They had established that Mr. Webb had had several episodes like this over the last few weeks, that they tended to last 10–20 minutes and resolved spontaneously.

Mr. Webb was looking much improved.

Dr. Caldwell said, "You look like you're feeling quite a bit calmer now."

"Yeah, very much. I'm still a little nervous but I think it has passed, Doc."

"That's good. Also, things look quite good in other ways. Your heart looks fine on the electrocardiogram. You have what is called tachycardia, meaning that your heart is beating quickly, but that is probably because you were very nervous and were hyperventilating.

"I didn't have a heart attack?"

Dr. Caldwell was reassuring, "No, Mr. Webb. You didn't have a heart attack, although we still have some tests to get back. As far as we can tell from your electrocardiogram your heart looks quite strong. What we think you had was a panic attack."

Mr. Webb replied, "Panic about what? I wasn't afraid of anything. I got afraid after it started."

"I understand, Mr. Webb. Panic attacks like this just happen to people. They can come out of the blue. When people have them they are afraid they are going to die. They think their heart is going to stop or that they are having a stroke. Panic attacks are a terrible thing to experience and they are very frightening for people. Fortunately, and most importantly, although they are very scary, they actually don't hurt you. Dr. Harrington, who is a psychiatrist, is going to come down here and see you in the emergency room and talk to you about this."

"A psychiatrist? Are you saying this is all in my head?"

"No, not exactly Mr. Webb. Panic attacks probably have a physical basis, but psychiatrists treat many illnesses now that have a physical basis, and there are medications and forms of counseling that can be used to treat panic attacks. Why don't you wait and talk to Dr. Harrington? He's a nice guy, I think you'll like him, and I think he can explain all of this to you."

☐ Discussion

The episodes experienced by this individual appear to satisfy criteria for panic attacks. This individual has become quite concerned about the possibility of having another episode and fears that he may be having a heart attack. We do not have clear evidence of agoraphobia or any evidence that some drug or medical condition is causally involved. Also, we do not have evidence for another specific Axis I disorder such as social phobia. This case appears to represent a clear, straightforward panic disorder.

For those with panic disorder, the frequency of attacks varies dramatically and the course can vary over time. For example, an individual may have several episodes clustered into a few days or a week followed by a period of time of weeks or months when they are panic free. Many times individuals with panic disorder fear that something medically is wrong with them, or that they are losing their minds. Because of the fears of further attacks, many individuals are bothered by anxiety on an ongoing basis.

Comorbidly, many patients with panic also have major depressive disorder or another anxiety disorder, and in evaluating a patient with panic it is always important to carefully screen the individual for any evidence of depression or any other anxiety disorder (social phobia, obsessive-compulsive disorder, generalized anxiety disorder, and specific phobias).

Of interest, although there is no specific laboratory tests for panic, it can be induced in those at risk using various paradigms including intravenous infusion of sodium lactate, a maneuver that rarely results in the induction of panic in "normals." This suggests some underlying biological proclivity towards developing panic in some individuals.

Lifetime prevalence rates for the disorder average around 2%. Panic is more common in women than men. Also, there is a strong familial tendency toward this disorder and twin studies suggest that there is clearly a genetic component for panic, although the specific gene or genes involved have not been isolated.

The treatments for panic disorder have evolved considerably in the last two decades. There are a number of medications that are effective in blocking panic attacks including anxiolytic drugs such as the benzodiazepines and antidepressant drugs such as the serotonin reuptake inhibitors. Structured manual based forms of psychotherapy for panic have also been developed, many utilizing cognitive behavioral approaches. These are relatively brief in duration, but can result in significant and lasting benefits.

☐ Questions for Further Discussion

1) Why do many people with panic develop agoraphobia?
2) Why do you think that individuals with one type of anxiety disorder are at higher risk for having another anxiety disorder comorbidly?

☐ References

American Psychiatric Association. (1994). *Diagnostic and statistical manual of mental disorders* (4th ed.). Washington, DC: Author.

☐ Suggested Readings

Coplan, J. D., & Lydiard, R. B. (1998). Brain circuits in panic disorder. *Biological Psychiatry, 44*, 1264–1276.

Davidson, J. R. (1998). The long-term treatment of panic disorder. *Journal of Clinical Psychiatry, 59*, 17–21.

den Boer, J. A. (1998). Pharmacotherapy of panic disorder: Differential efficacy from a clinical viewpoint. *Journal of Clinical Psychiatry, 59*, 30–36.

den Boer, J. A., & Slaap, B. R. (1998). Review of current treatment in panic disorder. *International Clinical Psychopharmacology, 13*, S25–S30.

Gelder, M. G. (1998). Combined pharmacotherapy and cognitive behavior therapy in the treatment of panic disorder. *Journal of Clinical Psychopharmacology, 18*, 2S–5S.

Goddard, A. W., & Charney, D. S. (1998). SSRIs in the treatment of panic disorder. *Depression and Anxiety, 1*, 114–120.

Griez, E., & Schruers, K. (1998). Experimental pathophysiology of panic. *Journal of Psychosomatic Research, 45*, 493–503.

Hofmann, S. G., & Spiegel, D. A. (1999). Panic control treatment and its applications. *Journal of Psychotherapy Practice and Research, 8*, 3–11.

Katschnig, H., & Amering, M. (1998). The long-term course of panic disorder and its predictors. *Journal of Clinical Psychopharmacology, 18*, 6S–11S.

Lecrubier, Y. (1998). The impact of comorbidity on the treatment of panic disorder. *Journal of Clinical Psychiatry, 59*, 11–14.

Ollendick, T. H. (1998). Panic disorder in children and adolescents: New developments, new directions. *Journal of Clinical Child Psychology, 27*, 234–245.

Rickels, K., & Schweizer, E. (1998). Panic disorder: Long-term pharmacotherapy and discontinuation. *Journal of Clinical Psychopharmacology, 18*, 12S–18S, 1998.

Roy-Byrne, P. P., & Cowley, D. S. (1994). Course and outcome in panic disorder: A review of recent follow-up studies. *Anxiety, 1*, 151–160.

Roy-Byrne, P. P., & Cowley, D. S. (1998). Search for pathophysiology of panic disorder. *Lancet, 352*, 1646–1647.

Sansone, R. A., Sansone, L. A., & Righter, E. L. (1998). Panic disorder: The ultimate anxiety. *Journal of Women's Health, 7*, 983–989.

Shear, M. K. (1995). Psychotherapy for panic disorder. *Psychiatric Quarterly, 66*, 321–328.

Sheehan, D. V., & Harnett-Sheehan, K. (1996). The role of SSRIs in panic disorder. *Journal of Clinical Psychiatry, 10*, 51–58.

Stein, D. J., & Bouwer, C. (1997). A neuro-evolutionary approach to the anxiety disorders. *Journal of Anxiety Disorders, 11,* 409–429.

Stoudemire, A. (1996). Epidemiology and psychopharmacology of anxiety in medical patients. *Journal of Clinical Psychiatry, 57,* 64–75.

Vanin, J. R., & Vanin, S. K. (1999). Blocking the cycle of panic disorder. Ways to gain control of the fear of fear. *Postgraduate Medicine, 105,* 141–146, 1999.

Westenberg, H. G., & Den Boer, J. A. (1993). New findings in the treatment of panic disorder. *Pharmacopsychiatry, 26,* 30–33.

CHAPTER

Obsessive-Compulsive Disorder

☐ Introduction

The essential features of this condition are the presence of obsessions (recurrent intrusive thoughts) that are upsetting to the individual, compulsions (repetitive, ritualistic behaviors that the individual cannot resist doing when they occur to him or her), or both. According to the DSM-IV, individuals with these conditions must at some time recognize that their thoughts and behaviors are unreasonable and excessive, although recent research indicates that some individuals lack this insight. The symptoms must cause marked distress, interfere with the person's functioning, or be time-consuming (defined as consuming an hour or more of time each day in the DSM-IV).

In the vignettes that follow, consider the following points:

1) List all the specific obsessions and compulsions of this person.
2) We have evidence that this person had some obsessive-compulsive traits earlier in life but that they later develop full-blown obsessive-compulsive disorder (OCD). When did this transition occur, and why might it have occurred at that point?
3) Elizabeth is spending a lot of time studying but is still failing academically. How can we explain this?

☐ **Diagnostic Criteria**
(DSM-IV)

A. Either obsessions or compulsions:

Obsessions as defined by 1, 2, 3, and 4:
1) Recurrent and persistent thoughts, impulses, or images that are experienced, at some time during the disturbance, as intrusive and inappropriate, and that cause marked anxiety or distress.
2) The thoughts, impulses, or images are not simply excessive worries about real-life problems.
3) The person attempts to ignore or suppress such thoughts, impulses, or images, or to neutralize them with some other thought or action.
4) The person recognizes that the obsessive thoughts, impulses, or images are a product of his or her own mind (not imposed from without as in thought insertion)

Compulsions as defined by 1 and 2:
1) Repetitive behaviors (hand washing, ordering, checking) or mental acts (e.g., praying, counting, repeating words silently) that the person feels driven to perform in response to an obsession, or according to rules that must be applied rigidly.
2) The behaviors or mental acts are aimed at preventing or reducing distress or preventing some dreaded event or situation; however, these behaviors or mental acts either are not connected in a realistic way with what they are designed to neutralize or prevent or are clearly excessive.

B. At some point during the course of the disorder, the person has recognized that the obsessions or compulsions are excessive or unreasonable. **Note:** This does not apply to children.
C. The obsessions or compulsions cause marked distress, are time consuming (take more than one hour a day), or significantly interfere with the person's normal routine, occupational (or academic) functioning, or usual social activities or relationships.
D. If another Axis I disorder is present, the content of the obsessions or compulsions is not restricted to it (e.g., preoccupation with food in the presence of an Eating Disorder, hair pulling in the presence of Trichotillomania; concern with appearance in the presence of Body Dysmorphic Disorder; preoccupation with drugs in the presence of a Substance Use Disorder; preoccupation with having a serious illness in the presence of Hypochondriasis; preoccupation with sexual urges or fantasies in the presence of a Para-

philia; or guilty ruminations in the presence of Major Depressive Disorder).

E. The disturbance is not due to the direct physiological effects of a substance (e.g., a drug of abuse, a medication) or a general medical condition.

☐ The Stories

I

Elizabeth Blake, was in her second year, studying plant biology at the University of Wisconsin. An excellent student, she had been valedictorian of her high school class in Hayward, Wisconsin, a small resort community surrounded by pine covered hills and fishing lakes in northwestern Wisconsin. Her father and mother ran a resort on one such lake, Moose Lake. She had had a fairly normal childhood, although she had always been known by her family as neat, and was described by her high school teachers as a perfectionist.

Early in high school, she developed a pattern of needing to touch certain things in a symmetrical fashion, whenever she thought about it. She would need to touch once to the left, once to the right, twice to the left inside the first tap, twice to the right inside the second tap, and then three taps in the middle. She might do this when sitting at a table by tapping her fingers in front of her, or she might do it in the air by waving her fingers. Sometimes she found that when she was in enclosed spaces such as a car she would have to make the touching ritual involve the left door and the right door with the intermediate strokes in between in the air. Whenever it occurred to her to do the ritual, she did it because she found herself very anxious until she did so. She realized it was kind of weird, and it bothered her sometimes because sometimes she had to do it in situations where it might draw attention to herself, for example when she was with family or friends. She was generally able to disguise it so that people did not know she was doing it.

From a very early age she also had been very concerned about cleanliness, living in an environment that was far from surgically clean, with the scent of pine as often as not mixed with the scent of fish or motor oil for much of her childhood. Unlike her older sister Gwen, she had never really enjoyed the resort activities. Most were too dirty or too grungy. She rarely fished, didn't particularly like to water ski, and tended to be bookish, which was fine with her family. Her need for cleanliness, however, bothered them. Throughout high school many times she would take two showers a day, one in the morning before school and one in the afternoon when she would get home. Sometimes she gave the excuse that she had not been able to shower after gym class, but it happened so frequently that her parents at times discussed it between themselves. They didn't mention it to her, thinking it was a decision that was up to her.

Toward the end of high school she was engaged in a contest with another student for the top position academically in the class. Her parents attributed the stress associated with this to some other odd behaviors that she developed in her senior year. Most of these involved needing to wash her hands several times a day, particularly whenever she touched food or touched doorknobs. Her parents were surprised by the amount of time she would spend washing her hands, and at the dry, cracked appearance of them. Before graduation she also developed the habit of washing the silverware she would be using immediately before dinner, and she took an inordinate amount of time to do so, frequently delaying the family's meal by 10 or 15 minutes. Her parents were tolerant, and saw this as evidence of her stress. Occasionally they remarked about it, her father sometimes kidding her about it, but nonetheless they tolerated it and life went on. When she met her goal and graduated first in her class, however, they became more concerned, in that she still seemed under a great deal of stress, and as if the award was then unimportant.

Since going to the University of Wisconsin, she continued many of these behaviors. They were noticed frequently by her roommate, Jessica Bellows, also from Hayward, a high school friend whose personality was very different than Elizabeth's. Jessica was outgoing, in some ways flamboyant. She was a theatre major, and her propensity for acting often emerged outside of the theatre. Elizabeth found her a great deal of fun because of this, and Jessica liked Elizabeth's predictability and stability. They had gotten along well in high school, and initially in college.

Over the course of the first year, however, Elizabeth's behaviors began to grate on Jessica. Jessica was not a particularly neat person, and she found Elizabeth's need for the room to be immaculate frustrating and eventually anger-provoking. She would return to their dorm room and find that Elizabeth had straightened not only her own things but Jessica's things as well. At first amazed, she then became worried when she saw the extremely neat piles of clothes carefully arranged in all of Elizabeth's drawers. One day she went into Elizabeth's closet to borrow a sweater when Elizabeth wasn't there, and was surprised to find that everything in the closet was hanging with equal distances between all the hangers. She was so impressed by the symmetry of the pattern that she got a ruler out of her desk, and was able to measure that each of the hanger tops were exactly 4 inches apart, all along the rod. She shook her head (This is weird.).

She also became increasingly estranged from Elizabeth for other reasons. For example, Elizabeth never wanted to go to the movies, or out for something to eat. She was always in the library studying, and would come back to the dorm room late at night, shower—for the second or third time that day—straighten everything in the room, and then go to bed. Jessica noticed that Elizabeth seemed tired and withdrawn and was not seeing any of the friends that the two of them had enjoyed the year before. She seemed to show no interest in dating. Then one evening she overheard a phone conversation between Elizabeth and her parents back in Hayward. Her parents were very concerned about Elizabeth's school work. Although the first year she had demonstrated the same academic success she enjoyed in high school, things had slipped this year and at the end of the first quarter they had received a note from Elizabeth indicating that she was being placed on academic probation. On the phone Elizabeth explained that she was having trouble getting things done. That it was hard for her to finish, and that she always saw the need to make small adjustments in papers she was writing before she turned them in, which frequently resulted in their being turned in late, if at all.

Jessica was at the end of her rope. One night she confronted Elizabeth about her concerns. Elizabeth became uncharacteristically angry and yelled that Jessica did not know what she was saying. Afterward, Elizabeth broke down in tears. Jessica told Elizabeth that she should be seen at the student health center and that she would be glad to go with her to see about getting help for the problems she was having. Maybe she was depressed? Maybe it was something else? The doctors there could help. Elizabeth replied, "The problem is not my mood, my problem is that I am failing to get anything done. I will never be able to be successful." (I am losing my mind.).

II

Elizabeth got out of bed early on Saturday morning. She had set her alarm for 6:00. Jessica was home for the weekend and Elizabeth had much to get done in her absence. First, she had to shower. It was important to get to the bathroom in the dormitory early before the others were up, so that her showering rituals would not be noticed. Pulling on a robe and grabbing her shampoo and soap she headed down the hall. Pushing open the women's bathroom door, she saw that the light was still off, meaning that no one was in the bathroom area. Turning on the light she crossed through the area containing the sinks and headed into the shower area. She went to the farthest shower in the corner, opened the curtain, and began inspecting the walls. The showers were always cleaned at the end of the day, but they were never clean enough. She was sure that all kinds of bad germs were lurking on the floor. First she ran the shower for a few minutes to get the floor wet and then, using a paper towel and soap scrubbed the bottom of the shower, beginning in the far right corner and working her way counterclockwise around the floor of the shower. She repeated this pattern ten times, felt satisfied that the surface was reasonably clean (although it could never be clean enough), started the shower again and carefully rinsed the floor. She took off her clothes and entered the shower. After getting wet she began her second ritual of the morning. This involved washing specific body parts a certain number of times in a certain sequence. The whole ritual took about 45 minutes.

By 7:30 she was back in her room. It was time to straighten things. A quick perusal of the room told her that she had her work cut out for her. Everything was a mess. Obtaining the 18 inch ruler from her desk, she began to carefully measure out the distance between the hangers. It was important that each item be four inches apart. Some particularly bulky items that wouldn't fit this pattern were placed at the right end of the rod six inches apart, but to be considered an exception an item had to be quite bulky. While doing this her thoughts drifted to Jessica, back in Hayward for the weekend. A sudden thought sprang into her mind (I get angry at Jessica sometimes. Really, really angry. Maybe sometime I'll hurt her or even kill her. I'll lose my temper, throw something at her, or hit her over the head with something like a bookend and kill her. There'll be blood all over the room. I'll go to jail. Oh my God.). This thought frightened and sickened her. At that point she began her touching ritual on the top of the bar. One tap to the left, one to the right, twice to left inside the first tap, twice on the right inside the second tap, and then three taps in the middle. She repeated this ten times and as she did so she noticed her anxiety diminished. (This is stupid, but I have to do it.) She returned to the task at hand, arranging her clothes.

☐ Discussion

Elizabeth seems to have both obsessions (e.g., her fear of dirt) and compulsions (e.g., washing her hands, showering frequently, the tapping ritual she performs). She understands that these are unreasonable, but feels unable to stop them. She is distressed by her symptoms. We're not sure how much total time she spends engaging in these thoughts and behaviors, but we do know that she is suffering academically. We have no evidence of an associated Axis I disorder, or that her problems are the effect of a drug or underlying medical condition.

Obsessions can take various forms in OCD. They can be thoughts, ideas, impulses, or images that intrude into the individual's consciousness. They are often referred to as "egodystonic," because the individual recognizes them as odd or unusual, and would like to be rid of them, but can't seem to do so. As in the current scenario, fears of contamination are quite common among individuals with this condition as is the need for symmetry (as in this individual's clothes arrangement in her closet).

Compulsions can also take various forms including checking behavior, hand washing, arranging or ordering things, or the performance of mental acts (e.g., counting, repeating phrases). It is not uncommon for someone with OCD to spend four or more hours a day engaged in these behaviors, and the symptoms can be quite debilitating.

The lifetime prevalence of obsessive-compulsive disorder is approximately 2–3%. It occurs equally in men and women (although men are usually more socially impaired). The course is usually characterized by waxing and waning, although the likelihood of full remission is low. Studies suggest that OCD does cluster in families and also is more common in the relatives of those with Tourette's Syndrome. OCD is commonly seen in conjunction with major depressive disorder and other anxiety disorders, and in the differential diagnosis one must consider other anxiety disorders. OCD can be confused with body dysmorphic disorder, where the preoccupation is with one's physical experience. In generalized anxiety disorder excessive worrying is present rather than obsessions. Major depressive disorder patients can frequently obsess or ruminate about their situation as well, but the obsessing in this disorder is not egodystonic.

A variety of treatments have been developed for obsessive-compulsive disorder. The first pharmacotherapy agent demonstrated to have efficacy for this condition was clomipramine, an antidepressant. Basic pharmacology studies demonstrated that the primary mechanism of action of clomipramine was reuptake inhibition of serotonin in neurons in the central nervous system. When the selected serotonin reuptake inhibitors (such as fluoxetine) became available they also were used for OCD and found to have efficacy. This has lead to considerable speculation that the underlying pathophysiology of obsessive compulsive disorder may involve the serotonin neurotransmitter system. While these drugs are quite helpful for many patients with OCD, they rarely result in complete elimination of all symptoms, and the residual symptoms are usually difficult to treat.

Various behavioral and cognitive behavioral psychotherapy approaches also have been developed, some of which are manual based. An optimal treatment for many patients may be a combination of a manual based behavioral psychotherapy with an antidepressant that targets the serotonin system.

☐ Questions for Further Discussion

1) Being somewhat obsessive and compulsive seems to characterize many successful people. How can we know when these traits cease being functional and become pathological?
2) If we treat people for obsessive-compulsive symptoms, is it possible they will be less productive?

☐ References

American Psychiatric Association. (1994). *Diagnostic and statistical manual of mental disorders* (4th ed.). Washington, DC: Author.

☐ Suggested Readings

Calamari, J. E., Wiegartz, P. S., & Janeck, A. S. (1999). Obsessive-compulsive disorder subgroups: A symptom-based clustering approach. *Behavior Research Therapy, 37,* 113–125.

Eisen, J. L., Goodman, W. K., Keller, M. B., Warshaw, M. G., DeMarco, L. M., Luce, D. D., & Rasmussen, S. A. (1999). Patterns of remission and relapse in obsessive-compulsive disorder: A 2-year prospective study. *Journal of Clinical Psychiatry, 60,* 346–361; quiz 352.

Gorman, J. M., & Kent, J. M. (1999). SSRIs and SMRIs: Broad spectrum of efficacy beyond major depression. *Journal of Clinical Psychiatry, 4,* 33–38.

Gornay, K. (1998). Obsessive-compulsive disorder: Nature and treatment. *Nursing Standards, 13,* 46–52, 53–54.

Kmmelkamp, P. M., Kraaijkamp, H. J., & van den Hout, M. A. (1999). Assessment of obsessive-compulsive disorder. *Behavior Modification, 23,* 269–279.

Leonard, H. (1999). Childhood onset obsessive-compulsive disorder: Is there a unique subtype? *Medicine and Health Rhode Island, 82,* 122.

O'Connor, K., Todorov, C., Robillard, S., Borgeat, F., & Brault, M. (1999). Cognitive behaviour therapy and medication in the treatment of obsessive-compulsive disorder: A controlled study. *Canadian Journal of Psychiatry, 44,* 64–71.

Pigott, T. A., & Seay, S. M. (1999). A review of the efficacy of selective serotonin reuptake inhibitors in obsessive-compulsive disorder. *Journal of Clinical Psychiatry, 60,* 101–106.

Skoog, G., & Skoog, I. (1999). A 40-year follow-up of patients with obsessive-compulsive disorder. *Archives of General Psychiatry, 56,* 121–127.

Sobin, C., Blundell, M., Weiller, F., Gavigan, C., Haiman, C., & Karayiorgou, M. (1999). Phenotypic characteristics of obsessive-compulsive disorder ascertained in adulthood. *Journal of Psychiatric Research, 33,* 265–273 .

12

CHAPTER

Social Phobia

☐ Introduction

Social phobia is basically characterized by anxiety and fear concerning social situations, such as being around other people (e.g., a party) or needing to perform in some way in front of others. Although only recently identified as a separate disorder, prevalence rates suggest social phobia is quite common and tends to cluster in families.

In reading the following scenarios, consider these issues:

1) Is there any evidence for a precipitating event having been associated with the onset of the disorder in this case?
2) What specifically does this individual fear will happen in social situations?
3) Does this problem interfere with this individual's functioning, social activities, or relationships?

☐ Diagnostic Criteria
(DSM-IV)

A. A marked and persistent fear of one or more social or performance situations in which the person is exposed to unfamiliar people or to possible scrutiny by others. The individual fears that he or she will act in a way (or show anxiety symptoms) that will be humiliating or embarrassing. **Note:** In children, there must be evidence of the capacity for age-appropriate social relationships with familiar people and the anxiety must occur in peer settings, not just in interactions with adults.

B. Exposure to the feared social situation almost invariably provokes anxiety, which may take the form of a situationally bound or situationally predisposed Panic Attack. **Note:** In children, the anxiety may be expressed by crying, tantrums, freezing, or shrinking from social situations with unfamiliar people.

C. The person recognizes that the fear is excessive or unreasonable. **Note:** In children, this feature may be absent.

D. The feared social or performance situations are avoided or else are endured with intense anxiety or distress.

E. The avoidance, anxious anticipation, or distress in the feared social or performance situations(s) interferes significantly with the person's normal routine, occupational (academic) functioning, or social activities or relationships, or there is marked distress about having the phobia.

F. In individuals under age 18 years, the duration is at least six months.

G. The fear or avoidance is not due to the direct physiological effects of a substance (e.g., a drug of abuse, a medication) or a general medical condition and is not better accounted for by another mental disorder (e.g., Panic Disorder with or without Agoraphobia, Separation Anxiety Disorder, Body Dysmorphic Disorder, a Pervasive Developmental Disorder, or Schizoid Personality Disorder).

H. If a general medical condition or another mental disorder is present, the fear in Criterion A is unrelated to it, e.g., the fear is not of stuttering, trembling in Parkinson's disease, or exhibiting abnormal eating behavior in Anorexia Nervosa or Bulimia Nervosa.

☐ The Stories

I

Larry Butler and John Edwards had been friends in high school. They had run track together, often double dated, traversed many of the crises of adolescence in tandem, and had remained supportive, good friends. It was only logical that they would room together their first year at the large state university in their home state in the upper midwest. The first few weeks of college were predictably anxiety-provoking. Would they be able to make it? How hard was it going to be? Would people like them? Within a period of a few months, both had settled into a predictable routine, and both were doing reasonably well in their classes, and dating. The two decided to pledge a fraternity together so that they could live together the next year as well, in a fraternity house.

Recently Larry had become increasingly concerned about John. To all outward appearances John seemed fine, but he didn't seem to want to go out much anymore or do things with Larry or his other friends. He tended to isolate himself in their dormitory room. Though he had initially seemed to enjoy campus activities and fraternity parties, he quit going out much at all, and Larry didn't understand why.

That night as both were crawling into their beds after an evening of study, Larry brought up his concern with John: "Man, I don't understand what's going on. Now you're talking about depledging and staying here in the dorm. What's the deal?"

John replied that the fraternity wasn't working out for him the way he had hoped, that he didn't think it was as much fun as he thought, and he'd like to spend more time alone.

"That's not like you at all, man" replied Larry. "Are you depressed, man? I really don't get you. And there's something that I've been wanting to talk to you about, but I've been afraid to because I know you're going to say no. I found out where you and I and some of the gang can get jobs working at a national park for the summer. Nobody really wants to go home. These jobs are pretty easy to get. Tom Peterson called and found out about it. We need to apply soon, and we could be at Yellowstone Park this summer rooming with other guys and girls. It would be one long party. Think of the backpacking, man. We would have a blast. But I bet you won't do it."

"And what about Sue?" Larry continued. "You haven't called her in three weeks. That chick really likes you, man. She's a neat girl. She really cares about you and now you've just dumped her. I don't understand you at all. You're weird."

The phone in the room rang and Larry picked it up. "Larry and John's room; fire away." John saw Larry's face tighten. Larry covered the mouthpiece with his hand, "Speak of the devil. It's Sue." John's heart sank. He had known this would happen but he wanted to put it off as long as possible.

Larry said, "Look man, this is your last chance. I'm going down to the T.V. room." He passed the phone to John and headed out the door.

John didn't know what to say. He thought Sue was a wonderful girl, but he knew she realized that he was a dope and that eventually she would get rid of him. He just couldn't face that. He swallowed hard and put the telephone to his ear and said, "Hi Sue. How are you doing?"

Sue replied, "Oh fine, John, how are you?"

His heart was in his throat. He thought she was such a nice person he was afraid he was going to offend her (Why is she calling? She could date anybody. She could have any guy she wanted. Why would she call me?).

"John, I wanted to see if you had notes from sociology class last Monday. I got tied up and didn't make it and haven't been able to get any notes from the class. With the test coming up and all I thought I should get a copy of them."

(That's why she called, she wants my notes. I knew she probably really didn't want to talk to me.)

"Sure Sue. I've got them. I can Xerox them and give them to you at class tomorrow."

"Or we could get together and have coffee or something and you could give them to me then." suggested Sue.

"I'm pretty busy tonight, Sue. I've got some stuff going on that I have to do. Why don't I give them to you in class tomorrow."

"Sure, well, okay. I look forward to seeing you then. Oh, by the way, I also wanted to tell you about something that is coming up. The sorority is going to have a Sadie Hawkins dance in two weeks, you know where the girl invites the guy. I was kind of wondering if you might be able to get free and go. It's on the 17th. It should be a lot of fun."

"Um . . . um . . . um . . . Can I talk to you tomorrow about it at class?"

"Sure," replied Sue, "I guess I'll see you then. Take care."

II

John Edwards, age 19, more then halfway through his freshman year at the state university, found that things were changing for him. It had started about four months ago when he had to drop a speech class. The anticipation of getting up in front of his classmates and delivering a 20 minute speech was simply too much. He had agonized over the speech for weeks. He was sure that people would think he was crazy because he would get up and shake and stumble over his words and do a terrible job. People would think he was weird. However, it wasn't just the speech. It was everything else as well. He didn't seem to know how to talk to people anymore. He'd say stupid things. He was awkward. People saw him as awkward. He didn't like to get to class early or stay after because he was afraid he would have to talk to friends and he always felt like he said the wrong thing.

Mainly he said things that were stupid and awkward. He couldn't remember if he had always been this stupid, or if this had just happened. He found he didn't want to be around people.

He and Larry had always met friends in the dormitory cafeteria for dinner. It was the social highlight of the day. These had always been great times. There were about eight or nine of them that would meet to eat together, tell stories of the day, talk about their classmates, tell jokes, and make plans for the weekend. John had been surprised how easy the transition to college had been for him, how he seemed to "fit in." But now all of that had evaporated.

Fraternity parties had become particularly difficult for him. The house he had pledged had parties every other weekend for house members and pledges. He found that he just couldn't make himself go anymore. He would worry about the upcoming parties continuously, have fantasies about the stupid things he would say, the awkward way he would look. He feared that he would not be able to talk with people, that they would find him stupid. He just couldn't force himself to go any longer.

The idea of working at Yellowstone Park on some level sounded wonderful, but he knew it involved meeting many new people, both men and women, and having to socialize, and he just didn't want to do it. He realized that all of this was crazy, but he still worried too much about these things.

He started thinking about his phone conversation earlier that evening with Sue. (What an utter dolt I was. I can't believe how stupid I am on the phone. I've really blown it now. She wanted my notes and then she asked me to that dance. I think she's just trying to be nice. I wonder. Nobody like Sue could like somebody like me. I have to be realistic about this. What would I do at the dance? I would have to meet all of Sue's sorority sisters. I'd have to talk to so many people. It would be going on for hours. I can't dance. I look weird when I try to dance. People might even laugh at me since I look so weird. I just can't go. I just couldn't stand it. I've just got to tell Sue that it's over.)

☐ Discussion

In this scenario, John clearly has marked fears about social situations involving the fraternity, the possible party at the sorority house, and fear of new situations such as the people he would have to meet if he took a summer job with his friend. He feels that he will act in embarrassing ways and end up being humiliated. We have evidence that he realizes the fear is unreasonable, and that he attempts to avoid these situations. We also have evidence at this point that this is affecting his relationships (with his friend, with Sue), his social activities, and that it is quite distressing to him. We have no evidence that it is secondary to the effect of some drug or a medical condition.

Social phobia is an interesting form of anxiety that was only recently added to the nomenclature. Such individuals may have fears about specific situations, or the fears may be generalized to most social situations. These individuals tend to have low self-esteem and feelings of inferiority, are very sensitive to what they perceive as criticism, and frequently perform poorly because of their level of anxiety.

Although prevalence estimates very dramatically, a lifetime prevalence of approximately 5% is a reasonable estimate. This disorder typically begins during the teenage years or can develop thereafter, and at times is associated with an acute precipitating event (in this case the speech class and the fear of giving the speech may have been the initiating event).

In the differential diagnosis, panic disorder and agoraphobia must be considered, although social phobia can be differentiated from agoraphobia without a history of panic disorder by the fact that social situations and scrutiny by others is the feared event. It must also be differentiated from common shyness or performance anxiety which can be normal traits.

Although systematic research on this condition has only recently developed, preliminary results suggest that certain forms of behavioral therapy as well as treatment with serotonin reuptake inhibitors may be effective in treating many individuals with this condition. Longitudinally it tends to wax and wane over time without treatment.

☐ Questions for Further Discussion

1) How can social phobia be differentiated from shyness?
2) Many people are afraid to perform or give a talk in front of a large number of people. Would this be considered social phobia?
3) Untreated, what would be the eventual consequences for John if he continued experiencing these symptoms?

☐ References

American Psychiatric Association. (1994). *Diagnostic and statistical manual of mental disorders* (4th ed.). Washington, DC: Author

☐ **Suggested Readings**

Barlow, D. H. (1994). Comorbidity in social phobia: Implications for cognitive-behavioral treatment. *Bulletin of the Menninger Clinic, 58,* A43–A57.

Beck, A. T. (1997). The past and future of cognitive therapy. *Journal of Psychotherapy Practice and Research, 6,* 276–284.

Clark, D. B., Feske, U., Masia, C. L., Spaulding, S. A., Brown, C., Mammen, O., & Shear, M. K. (1997). Systematic assessment of social phobia in clinical practice. *Depression and Anxiety, 6,* 47–61.

Den Boer, J. A., Van Vliet, I. M., & Westenberg, H. G. (1994). Recent advances in the psychopharmacology of social phobia. *Progress in Neuropsychopharmacology and Biological Psychiatry, 18,* 625–645.

Den Boer, J. A., Van Vliet, I. M., & Westenberger, H. G. (1995). Recent developments in the psychopharmacology of social phobia. *European Archives of Psychiatry and Clinical Neuroscience, 244,* 309–316.

Jefferson, J. W. (1995). Social phobia: A pharmacologic treatment overview. *Journal of Clinical Psychiatry,* 56: 18–24.

Jefferson, J. W. (1996). Social phobia: Everyone's disorder? *Journal of Clinical Psychiatry,* 57, 28–32.

Jefferys, D. (1997). Social phobia. The most common anxiety disorder. *Australian Family Physician, 26,* 1061–1067.

Liebowitz, M. R. (1993). Pharmacotherapy of social phobia. *Journal of Clinical Psychiatry, 54,* 31–35.

Merikangas, K. R., & Angst, J. (1995). Comorbidity and social phobia: Evidence from clinical, epidemiologic, and genetic studies. *European Archives of Psychiatry and Clinical Neuroscience, 244,* 297–303.

Miner, C. M., & Davidson, J. R. (1995). Biological characterization of social phobia. *European Archives of Psychiatry and Clinical Neuroscience, 244,* 304–308.

Stravynski, A., & Greenberg, D. (1998). The treatment of social phobia: A critical assessment. *Acta Psychiatrica Scandinavica, 98,* 171–181.

Tancer, M. E. (1993). Neurobiology of social phobia. *Journal of Clinical Psychiatry, 54,* 26–30.

CHAPTER

Post-traumatic Stress Disorder

☐ Introduction

Post-traumatic stress disorder (PTSD) occurs after an individual is exposed to an extremely traumatic event. Such events often involve actual or threatened death or injury. The person experiences the event with a sense of helplessness, intense fear, or even horror. Examples of possible precipitants of PTSD would include severe automobile accidents, being raped or assaulted, and being exposed to mortal combat or serving as a prisoner of war. The person then re-experiences the event in various ways. These include recurrent stressful recollections of the event, dreams of the event, and a sense that the traumatic event may be occurring again. Cues that were associated with the event may cause the symptoms to recur. The individual then attempts to avoid such cues in various ways. These may include a numbing of responses or becoming distant and removed. Individuals with PTSD also evidence symptoms of arousal, including irritability, hypervigilance, insomnia, and problems concentrating. Symptoms must last at least one month (and are characterized as chronic if they last more than three months), and must be accompanied by significant distress or impairment.

☐ Diagnostic Criteria
(DSM-IV)

A. The person has been exposed to a traumatic event in which both of the following were present:

1) The person experienced, witnessed, or was confronted with an event or events that involved actual or threatened death or serious injury, or a threat to the physical integrity of self or others.
2) The person's response involved intense fear, helplessness, or horror. **Note:** In children, this may be expressed instead by disorganized or agitated behavior.

B. The traumatic event is persistently re-experienced in one (or more) of the following ways:
1) Recurrent and intrusive distressing recollections of the event, including images, thoughts, or perceptions. **Note:** In young children, repetitive play may occur in which themes or aspects of the trauma are expressed.
2) Recurrent distressing dreams of the event. **Note:** In children, there may be frightening dreams without recognizable content.
3) Acting or feeling as if the traumatic event were recurring (includes a sense of reliving the experience, illusions, hallucinations, and dissociative flashback episodes, including those that occur upon awakening or when intoxicated). **Note:** In young children, trauma-specific reenactment may occur.
4) Intense psychological distress at exposure to internal or external cues that symbolize or resemble an aspect of the traumatic event.
5) Physiological reactivity on exposure to internal or external cues that symbolize or resemble an aspect of the traumatic event.

C. Persistent avoidance of stimuli associated with the trauma and numbing of general responsiveness (not present before the trauma), as indicated by three (or more) of the following:
1) Efforts to avoid thoughts, feelings, or conversations associated with the trauma.
2) Efforts to avoid activities, places, or people that arouse recollections of the trauma.
3) Inability to recall an important aspect of the trauma.
4) Markedly diminished interest or participation in significant activities.
5) Feelings of detachment or estrangement from others.
6) Restricted range of affect (e.g., unable to have loving feelings).
7) Sense of a foreshortened future (e.g., does not expect to have a career, marriage, children, or a normal life span).

D. Persistent symptoms of increased arousal (not present before the trauma), as indicated by two (or more) of the following:
1) Difficulty falling or staying asleep
2) Irritability or outbursts of anger

3) Difficulty concentrating
4) Hypervigilance
5) Exaggerated startle response
E. Duration of the disturbance (symptoms in Criteria B, C, and D) is more than one month.
F. The disturbance causes clinically significant distress or impairment in social, occupational, or other important areas of functioning.

☐ The Stories

I

Sarah Jackson sat in the parish house with Father Martin, her priest. She was trying to explain to him what had happened in her life and at the same time was trying to understand it herself. It was spring, and it had been a year since the flood. For reasons she didn't readily understand, her symptoms, which had gotten better during the winter, were returning. She was starting to feel the way she had felt the year before for several months after the flood. She was having trouble sleeping and having trouble concentrating as well. She kept having thoughts about the flood, and about the day she almost drown in her own basement. These thoughts would literally pop into her head, and she would ruminate about them. The dreams had come back as well. There were several versions, but in the most common one she was in a box (or was it a casket?) and the water started seeping into the bottom and getting higher and higher. When it got as high as her face she would wake up in a sweat.

The river levels had been rising this spring, as they did every year; she found it difficult to even look at the river. If she happened to glance at it, drove on a bridge over it, or even thought about it, she became very anxious. If anyone even mentioned the flood the previous year (and somebody always seemed to) she would become anxious and tremulous and the thoughts would intrude again. She didn't think she was depressed (or was she?), but she had become convinced by the idea that she would not live more than a few more years; that something would prevent her from living a normal life. Things were going to come to an end soon (I'm afraid something is going to happen to me.).

Father Martin listened attentively and nodded as she recollected these thoughts. "How much sleep are you getting Sarah?"

"Oh, probably three or four hours a night. I don't know. It seems like I spend a lot of time lying in bed looking at the ceiling."

Father Martin nodded, "Have you and Rick thought about moving away from the river, inland, so you wouldn't be exposed to it?"

"Oh, I've been after Rick to move since the flood, but we took such a terrible financial hit—you know we didn't buy flood insurance—that we couldn't afford to move now, and who would buy our house? It's in the flood plain now. No, I think we have to stay even though I'd rather live anywhere else. I think I'd prefer to live in the middle of the desert," she said and shyly smiled.

Father Martin asked, "Sarah, do you think maybe you're depressed? You know the treatments for depression work very well these days."

"No, Father, I don't think I'm depressed. I mean I feel down sometimes but I'm mainly just afraid and worried and I feel like my mind is out of my control. I actually feel kind of numb, like I'm in a cloud much of the time. I don't think I feel things the same as I used to. I feel kind of dull and thick."

Father Martin replied, "But you usually seem kind of anxious and irritable to me. I've noticed that change since the flood. You seem to always be worried about something, always afraid of something. I hate to see you this way, Sarah."

II

Sarah and Rick Jackson had moved into their house by the river 15 years before. Sarah loved the house. She loved to stand on the back deck and look out across the river to the golf course across the way on the Minnesota side. She prided herself on keeping a tidy house, and loved gardening. She had a small vegetable garden and raised annuals as well as beds of perennials. On days when she wasn't working as a waitress at the Family Diner she would be out in the backyard garden, weeding, arranging, and planting. Rick was a construction foreman and worked long hours, and because of his schedule they didn't have a lot of time together at home. Sundays were always their day together and on those days they would work in the garden after church, or go for a drive in the country, or sometimes go to Buffalo River State Park on the Minnesota side and hike a bit. Sarah was a pleasant, sensible, warm-hearted woman of 40; Rick, a gruff, outspoken, but ultimately kind and empathic, prematurely gray 42-year-old man. They had no children but kept a black and white stray dog, Proclus, they had obtained shortly after they had moved into the house. The dog was getting old now, suffered from arthritis, and sometimes had difficulty getting up and down the stairs.

It had been a terrible winter the year before, with record levels of snow—greater than 100 inches total—very atypical for the region. It had also been bitterly cold and windy, and all were much relieved when the snow melted and the earth started to warm.

The Red River on which they lived was somewhat unusual in that it flowed north into Canada, eventually dumping into a lake north of the city of Winnipeg. Well into the spring thaw the local news media started to express worries that there might be a problem with flooding. The Red River frequently flooded its banks but in the period Sarah and Rick had lived in their home it had never come close to reaching their yard, let alone their house. They were quite confident that they were well above any flood that might occur. However, they started to become increasingly concerned when reports from communities upriver such as Breckenridge, Minnesota indicated significant problems with flooding—flooded basements near the river and in some cases actual flooding of the streets in certain neighborhoods.

Predictions were that the rise in the river would be higher than normal. There was no way to know how high it would be. During those days Sarah would get up in the morning, stand on the back deck, gaze down the riverbank, and try to ascertain whether or not the river had come up during the night. More often than not, it had. She and Rick were becoming increasingly concerned. During the day she kept the radio tuned to a channel that would give the water levels every few minutes, and predictions about what would happen over the next few days. She had never seen the river this wide and this full of debris. Things would sweep by—pieces of wood, sometimes a picnic table, various other sundry things the river had captured in its course from the south.

The entire town was now waiting and holding its breath, hoping. On a Thursday afternoon a report came that the river would be peaking in probably three or four days. (At least the end is in sight.) She now found herself checking the water level several times a day. She had driven some stakes into the side of the riverbank—below the land dike that offered further protection—so that she could plot the progression of the water exactly. It continued to rise up the riverbank behind the dike, and by Saturday morning seemed almost level with the edge of their lawn. By that afternoon it was well across the lawn and up to the backyard deck. Sarah was getting increasingly frightened. Reluctantly, sadly, and fearfully she and Rick made preparations to move all their valuables out of the basement and first floor and onto the top level. They worked committedly and as quickly as they could, while the radio warned of the rising water. At 7:30 p.m. there was a report that the river may have peaked and they breathed a sigh of relief, but continued to move furniture and boxes and other things upstairs just in case. They were reassured by the 10:00 p.m. report on the news, and decided to go to bed.

Sarah slept fitfully until approximately 3:00 a.m. when she was awakened by someone pounding on the front door. She hurriedly pulled on her robe and attempted to turn on the lights but there was no electricity. She felt her way down the stairway and was horrified to hear the sound of rushing water in the basement below. She ran to the front door, threw it open, and saw a fireman standing outside yelling that there had been a break in the dike downtown and that water was coming into their neighborhood overland. They needed to evacuate their house. Sarah ran back to the foot of the stairs and yelled up for Rick. Just then a terrible sinking feeling came over her as she realized she had not moved the family photograph albums out of the basement. Without thinking, she plunged down the stairs, around the corner, and started down the final set of steps. She was horrified to find water in the basement, brown, dirty, dark, and swirling, pouring in through the casement windows. There was barely enough light for her to see, and on the table in the middle of the room just a few inches above the water were the albums. Impulsively she waded down the last few steps until the water was above her knees. She started across the room (My God, the water is so cold.), the water pushed against her as she walked, flooding through the basement. She leaned forward into the water which now was at thigh height, tripped over some object on the floor and fell forward into the water. Gasping and sputtering she regained her footing and glanced at the table. It was too late, the tabletop had disappeared and with it the albums. Rick was yelling for her at the top of the stairs. She turned and again started for the steps, again slipping and falling forward into the cold water. She was sure she was going to die. She can never remember being so cold, so scared, and so sure that her life was over. Rick came running down the steps, waded into the water, helped her regain her footing, and they started up the steps together.

☐ Discussion

Sarah clearly was involved in a very traumatic event. Of interest, the traumatic event occurred in two forms. The more chronic stress of the rising water, and the more acute stress of the episode in the basement when she goes to get the photograph albums. A third time of stress, not discussed in the chapter, would be the aftermath of the flood, and the impact on the couple financially, socially, and physically.

We know from her interview with Father Martin that she has recurrent intrusive thoughts and dreams about the event and when exposed to cues (seeing the river) reacts strongly. She has tried to avoid exposure to the river and conversations about it. She talks about feeling numb and detached. She has a sense that she will not live long. She is noted by Father Martin to be irritable and constantly worried (perhaps hypervigilant?). It is the symptom picture and history that suggest the diagnosis of post-traumatic stress disorder rather than another anxiety disorder. Individuals with post-traumatic stress disorder are at increased risk for depression and other anxiety disorders as well.

The prevalence of PTSD has varied widely in various surveys, and the exact prevalence in the community at large is not known. Generally, symptoms begin in the first three months after trauma, but they can be delayed many months or years.

As with many psychiatric conditions, there is a role for both medications and psychotherapy counseling for patients with PTSD. Both antidepressants and anxiolytic agents such as benzodiazepines may be useful, particularly if there are prominent symptoms of depression and anxiety. Structured forms of counseling, including those using cognitive behavioral approaches, also have been useful for individuals with PTSD.

☐ Questions for Further Discussion

1) This form of PTSD might be termed an Anniversary Reaction. Why?
2) Many people experienced the flood, but not all developed PTSD. What might put people at risk for this, or protect them from it?

☐ References

American Psychiatric Association. (1994). *Diagnostic and statistical manual of mental disorders* (4th ed.). Washington, DC: Author.

☐ Suggested Readings

Blaszczynski, A., Gordon, K., Silove, D., Sloane, D., Hillman, K., & Panasetis, P. (1998). Psychiatric morbidity following motor vehicle accidents: A review of methodological issues. *Comprehensive Psychiatry, 39,* 111–121.
Bremner, J. D. (1999). Does stress damage the brain? *Biological Psychiatry, 45,* 797–805.

Dunnegan, S. W. (1997). Violence, trauma, and substance abuse. *Journal of Psychoactive Drugs, 29*, 345–361.

Finnegan, A. P. (1998). Clinical assessment for post-traumatic stress disorder. *British Journal of Nursing, 7*, 212–218.

Golier, J., & Yehuda, R. (1998). Neuroendocrine activity and memory-related impairments in posttraumatic stress disorder. *Developmental Psychopathology, 10*, 857–869.

Jacobs, W. J., & Dalenberg, C. (1998). Subtle presentation of post-traumatic stress disorder. Diagnostic issues. *Psychiatric Clinics of North America, 21*, 835–845.

Leskin, G. A., Kaloupek, D. G., & Keane, T. M. (1998). Treatment for traumatic memories: Review and recommendations. *Clinical Psychology Review, 18*, 983–1001.

Meek, J. K., & Kablinger, A. (1998). Antidepressants and posttraumatic stress disorder. *Journal of Louisiana State Medical Society, 150*, 487–489.

Ouimette, P. C., Brown, P. J., & Najavits, L. M. (1998). Course and treatment of patients with both substance use and posttraumatic stress disorders. *Addictive Behavior, 23*, 785–795.

Peebles-Kleiger, M. J., & Zerbe, K. J. (1998). Office management of posttraumatic stress disorder. A clinician's guide to a pervasive problem. *Postgraduate Medicine, 103*, 181–196.

Rusch, M. D. (1998). Psychological response to trauma. *Plastic Surgery Nursing, 18*, 147–153.

Stevenson, J. (1999). The treatment of the long-term sequelae of child abuse. *Journal of Child Psychology and Psychiatry, 40*, 89–111.

Yehuda, R. (1999). Biological factors associated with susceptibility to posttraumatic stress disorder. *Canadian Journal of Psychiatry, 44*, 34–39.

Yehuda, R. (1998). Psychoneuroendocrinology of post-traumatic stress disorder. *Psychiatric Clinics of North America, 21*, 359–379.

14
CHAPTER

Generalized Anxiety Disorder

☐ Introduction

Generalized anxiety disorder (GAD) is a relatively recent addition to the official psychiatric nomenclature. The evolution of this diagnosis over the last few decades parallels a growing interest in anxiety disorders in general, both in terms of diagnostic classification and treatment development. In considering the following stories, remember that people with GAD have ongoing anxiety symptoms that often affect them in a variety of spheres. These may include specific physical symptoms (e.g., fatigue, muscle tension), cognitive symptoms (e.g., slowed thinking), and behavioral symptoms (e.g., pacing, being on edge).

In reading the following stories, notice several points:

1) As far as one can tell from the information provided, what has the history of this disorder been over this individual's lifetime? What was the age of onset, and what has been the longitudinal course?
2) To be a psychiatric disorder, symptoms must result in significant distress or impairment. Is this individual significantly distressed? In what way is he impaired by the illness?
3) This illness, as with many forms of psychopathology, not only disturbs the affected individual but also often has profound consequences for those in their environment. Please consider the degree to which this illness impacts on those around the affected individual, especially his wife and daughter.

☐ Diagnostic Criteria
(DSM-IV)

A. Excessive anxiety and worry (apprehensive expectation), occurring more days than not for at least six months, about a number of events or activities (such as work or school performance).
B. The person finds it difficult to control the worry.
C. The anxiety and worry are associated with three (or more) of the following six symptoms (with at least some symptoms present for more days than not for the past six months). **Note:** Only one item is required in children.
   1) Restlessness or feeling keyed up or on edge
   2) Being easily fatigued
   3) Difficulty concentrating or mind going blank
   4) Irritability
   5) Muscle tension
   6) Sleep disturbance (difficulty falling or staying asleep, or restless unsatisfying sleep)
D. The focus of the anxiety and worry is not about having a Panic Attack (as in Panic Disorder), being embarrassed in public (as in Social Phobia), being contaminated (as in Obsessive-Compulsive Disorder), being away from home or close relatives (as in Separation Anxiety Disorder), gaining weight (as in Anorexia Nervosa), having multiple physical complaints (as in Somatization Disorder), or having a serious illness (as in Hypochondriasis), and the anxiety and worry do not occur exclusively during Posttraumatic Stress Disorder.
E. The anxiety, worry, or physical symptoms cause clinically significant distress or impairment in social, occupational, or other important areas of functioning.
F. The disturbance is not due to the direct physiological effects of a substance (e.g., a drug of abuse, a medication) or a general medical condition (e.g., hyperhyroidism) and does not occur exclusively during a Mood Disorder, a Psychotic Disorder, or a Pervasive Developmental Disorder.

☐ The Stories

I

John Ford, a 43-year-old plumber who lived in Rockford, Illinois, should have been happy and proud, but his worrying ruined it all for himself.

His 22-year-old daughter, Jenny, was to be married in three weeks. She had just graduated from college and had done very well in school. He was very proud of her. She was marrying a young man who had been a classmate, someone John and his wife already cared about a great deal. His daughter was being launched, and they were having a big family wedding, but he could do nothing but worry. Now his worries were focused on the wedding. He had fantasies that the flowers wouldn't arrive, that somehow the reception wouldn't come off, that the food would be poor, that the band would get the date wrong and not show up, and that the weather would be bad and everyone would get rained on. He had talked to his wife, Mildred, about these issues repeatedly. At first she would try to reassure him but would then say, "John, don't worry so much. You're nothing but a worrywort. You always have been."

(She's right. I've always been a worrier my whole life. I can't seem to accept things and just let them happen. I worry about my job. I always think I'll make some mistake. I worry so much that it makes me sick. I have trouble sleeping. I feel tired all the time. I can't ever sit still. I have to pace. It drives me crazy to sit in a chair.)

Social situations like the wedding were particularly problematic for him, but he could worry about anything. He had a sense of dread whenever anything important would come up including something positive, like a new big job where his skills would be put to the test, or his daughter's wedding. He had a sense of dread that something was going to go wrong. When he worried he had difficulty remembering things or concentrating on things. His neck and back would feel tense.

He realized that he worried excessively but he had never been able to figure out a way to stop it. Sometimes it would get better and sometimes it would get worse, but it never went away completely. He had always worried about something bad happening to his wonderful daughter, and now he had begun to have fantasies that something dreadful would happen to her and her new husband on their honeymoon. (Why can't I just enjoy life and accept things like they are?)

John wasn't really sure when the problem started. It clearly had been well established during his high school years. John had been a pretty good basketball player, playing forward, but he spent most of his high school years as a substitute. His coach told him that he had good natural abilities but he never seemed to let himself go. He worried constantly about his performance and was inhibited to the point where it was hard for him to get caught up in the game and really throw himself into it. He also had great anxiety in any kind of testing situation and was very worried, despite the fact that he made above average grades, that at any point he might fail in school.

Even times that were relaxing for most people were difficult for John. This included family vacations. He, his wife, and daughter would take a driving trip somewhere every summer. He carefully planned these in advance, arranging for hotel rooms, and planning activities. He was always deathly afraid, however, that something would go wrong, that the car would break down (although it never did) or that his wife and daughter would not have a good enough time. He was afraid he would make a wrong turn. He never wanted to travel after dark fearing he would become lost and that this would endanger his family.

John was part owner of his own plumbing firm. He and his two partners frequently did jobs together and specialized in installing plumbing in new homes. Their group was known for being honest and prompt, but John's two partners would frequently kid him about getting pent up and having to go out and walk, at times leaving the job. They were fond of John and saw him as a good worker, but at times were somewhat upset by the fact that on certain days he would get so anxious he would have to leave the site and go home early. They tolerated this out of friendship and respect, but Bill, who he had known the longest, on several occasions had urged him to seek help for his anxiety, although he never had.

II

When Jenny returned from a bridal shower that some of her college roommates had thrown for her, she came and sat next to her father on the couch and put her hand on his arm. Mildred was in the kitchen fixing dinner, out of earshot.

"Dad, I need to talk to you about how things are going. You've gotten so jumpy again lately. I know that you are a worrier but it seems to be getting worse, about the wedding. Frankly, you're driving Mom crazy and it's starting to make me nervous as well. Things are going along fine. I don't think you need to worry this much about things. You need to just relax."

John felt ashamed that he was worrying his daughter. (Why did he do this to people? Why couldn't he just control himself?)

"I'm so sorry, Jenny. I want the wedding to be perfect for you. I just don't know what to do. I have this terrible sense that something is going to go wrong. I've always been this way. Sometimes I think it's getting better, but at times like this with the wedding coming up I know it's really gotten worse. I'll try very hard not to talk about it so much. I really don't want to upset you or your mother."

"Dad, you know what this reminds me of? Remember that time when you, Mom, and I were to go camping in Wisconsin? Do you remember, you got so nervous about everything. You were sure we were going to get lost. You were afraid the weather was going to turn bad and wash away our tent. You were afraid we would run out of food. You worried that a bear was going to get into the tent. You worried so much that we actually packed up and came home early. Remember that? Dad, it kind of ruined the vacation. I'm not saying this because I want you to feel bad, it's just that this wedding is very important to Mom and me and we need you to be there for us and help us."

At this point John was feeling horrible. As he looked back, his life seemed one long series of failures where he had let his wife and daughter down, unable to control himself and his thinking. (What's wrong with me. I think I need to see my doctor.)

☐ Discussion

John clearly has a disorder that has a significant impact on his functioning, his self-esteem, and his family. This disorder seems to have started during adolescence, and was present during his high school years. Because he states he feels out of control and he has several symptoms as required by criteria C, lacking only "irritability" of the six possible criteria.

In evaluating a person such as John, one must exclude other Axis I diagnoses for which anxiety can be a prominent symptom. Without access to the results of a detailed interview, these other disorders cannot be excluded completely. However, the information we have suggests that the anxiety problem is primary, generalized, and apparently not attributable to some other Axis I disorder. It also would be useful to take a complete history regarding any medication that John might be taking that might cause anxiety (e.g., stimulants for adult attention deficit disorder) and to make sure his physical status is not causal (e.g., overactive thyroid).

We also have no evidence of another Axis I anxiety disorder (panic disorder, social phobia, OCD). We have no evidence of multiple physical complaints or fears of having serious illnesses which would suggest somatization disorder or hypochondriasis.

Generalized anxiety disorder is an Axis I condition characterized by excessive anxiety and worry that occurs on the majority of days for a period of at least six months. It can begin in childhood or adolescence, but can also can develop in adulthood. The course is usually chronic, and fluctuating. Prevalence estimates indicate a lifetime rate of approximately 5%. Although increased anxiety does appear to run in families, specific clustering of generalized anxiety disorder has not been consistently reported.

Complications from GAD generally evolve from the psychosocial implications of having the disorder. For example, John works with colleagues who tend to be tolerant of his anxiety problems, and he has a family that is tolerant as well. Others may not be as fortunate and may have problems holding jobs or maintaining meaningful relationships because of ongoing problems with anxiety. Individuals with GAD may attribute their symptoms to underlying medical illnesses and may, therefore, have evaluations performed or be treated with medications that may themselves carry a risk.

Structured forms of psychotherapy have been developed for GAD, as have drug therapies.

☐ Questions for Further Discussion

1) Is anxiety always a problem? When might anxiety be helpful for him or others?
2) If you knew John, what would you suggest to him? Would you offer any advice?
3) Think about people you know. Do you know people like John? Or do you know people who never seem anxious?

☐ References

American Psychiatric Association. (1994). *Diagnostic and statistical manual of mental disorders* (4th ed.). Washington, DC: Author.

☐ Suggested Readings

Angst, J., & Vollrath, M. (1991). The natural history of anxiety disorders. *Acta Psychiatrica Scandinavica, 84,* 446–452.

Birmaher, B., Yelovich, A. K., & Renaud, J. (1998). Pharmacologic treatment for children and adolescents with anxiety disorders. *Pediatric Clinics of North America, 45,* 1187–1204.

Bradwejn, J. (1993). Benzodiazepines for the treatment of panic disorder and generalized anxiety disorder: Clinical issues and future directions. *Canadian Journal of Psychiatry, 38,* S109–S113.

Connor, K. M., & Davidson, J. R. (1998). Generalized anxiety disorder: Neurobiological and pharmacotherapeutic perspectives. *Biological Psychiatry, 44,* 1286–1294.

Emmanuel, J., Simmonds, S., & Tyrer, P. (1998). Systematic review of the outcome of anxiety and depressive disorders. *British Journal of Psychiatry Supplement, 34,* 35–41.

Lydiard, R. B., & Brawman-Mintzer, O. (1998). Anxious depression. *Journal of Clinical Psychiatry, 59,* 10–17.

Mintzer, J. E., & Brawman-Mintzer, O. (1996). Agitation as a possible expression of generalized anxiety disorder in demented elderly patients: Toward a treatment approach. *Journal of Clinical Psychiatry, 57,* 55–63.

Rickels, K., & Schweizer, E. (1998). The spectrum of generalized anxiety in clinical practice: The role of short-term, intermittent treatment. *British Journal of Psychiatry Supplement 34,* 49–54.

Robinson, M. D. (1993). Anxiety disorders in the general practice. *New Jersey Medicine, 90,* 129–132.

Teicher, M. H. (1998). Biology of anxiety. *Medical Clinics of North America, 72,* 791–814.

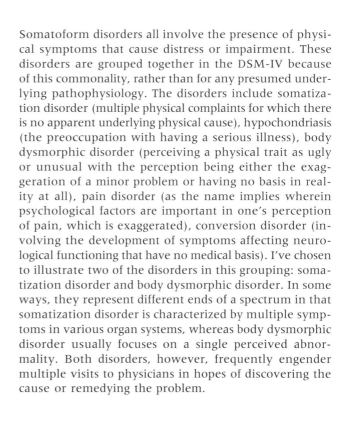

PART

VI SOMATOFORM DISORDERS

Somatoform disorders all involve the presence of physical symptoms that cause distress or impairment. These disorders are grouped together in the DSM-IV because of this commonality, rather than for any presumed underlying pathophysiology. The disorders include somatization disorder (multiple physical complaints for which there is no apparent underlying physical cause), hypochondriasis (the preoccupation with having a serious illness), body dysmorphic disorder (perceiving a physical trait as ugly or unusual with the perception being either the exaggeration of a minor problem or having no basis in reality at all), pain disorder (as the name implies wherein psychological factors are important in one's perception of pain, which is exaggerated), conversion disorder (involving the development of symptoms affecting neurological functioning that have no medical basis). I've chosen to illustrate two of the disorders in this grouping: somatization disorder and body dysmorphic disorder. In some ways, they represent different ends of a spectrum in that somatization disorder is characterized by multiple symptoms in various organ systems, whereas body dysmorphic disorder usually focuses on a single perceived abnormality. Both disorders, however, frequently engender multiple visits to physicians in hopes of discovering the cause or remedying the problem.

15
CHAPTER

Somatization Disorder

☐ Introduction

The following vignettes illustrate one of the somatoform disorders—somatization disorder. This disorder has been referred to in various ways over time including "hysteria" and "Briquette's syndrome," and is characterized by symptoms in various organ systems that lead people to repeatedly seek medical care, and have involved expensive, and at times dangerous evaluations and surgical procedures for which the outcomes are usually poor. In reading the following vignettes, please keep the following issues in mind:

1) How many different organ systems are involved?
2) Consider the nature of this patient's relationships with the various doctors whom she has seen, and in particular her relationship with her current physician, Dr. Gardner.
3) Pay attention to the way Dr. Gardner interacts with this patient. Is she confrontational or supportive? Is she abrupt or patient?
4) Is this woman just a complainer?

☐ Diagnostic Criteria
(DSM-IV)

A. A history of many physical complaints beginning before age 30 that occur over a period of several years and result in treatment being sought or significant impairment in social, occupational, or other important areas of functioning.

B. Each of the following criteria must have been met, with individual symptoms occurring at any time during the course of the disturbance:

1) *Four pain symptoms*: a history of pain related to at least four different sites or functions (e.g., head, abdomen, back, joints, extremities, chest, rectum, during menstruation, during sexual intercourse, or during urination).

2) *Two gastrointestinal symptoms*: a history of at least two gastrointestinal symptoms other than pain (e.g., nausea, bloating, vomiting other than during pregnancy, diarrhea, or intolerance of several different foods).

3) *One sexual symptom*: a history of at least one sexual or reproductive symptom other than pain (e.g., sexual indifference, erectile or ejaculatory dysfunction, irregular menses, excessive menstrual bleeding, vomiting throughout pregnancy).

4) *One pseudoneurological symptom*: a history of at least one symptom of deficit suggesting a neurological condition not limited to pain (conversion symptoms such as impaired coordination or balance, paralysis or localized weakness, difficulty swallowing or lump in throat, aphonia, urinary retention, hallucinations, loss of touch or pain sensation, double vision, blindness, deafness, seizures; disassociative symptoms such as amnesia; or loss of consciousness other than fainting).

C. Either 1) or 2):

1) After appropriate investigation, each of the symptoms in Criterion B cannot be fully explained by a known general medical condition or the direct effects of a substance (e.g., a drug of abuse, a medication).

2) When there is a related general medical condition, the physical complaints or resulting social or occupational impairment are in excess of what would be expected from the history, physical examination, or laboratory findings.

D. The symptoms are not intentionally produced or feigned (as in Factitious Disorder or Malingering).

☐ The Stories

I

Paul Billings was driving his wife Margaret to see their family physician, Dr. Gardner. It wasn't a long drive. Dr. Gardner and her colleagues in a family practice group were officed in a professional building near a shopping mall in the comfortable middle class suburb where Paul and Margaret lived. Paul certainly knew the way by heart. It seemed he had driven it a million times. Paul was really at his wits end. He didn't know what to do any longer. He had known his wife's health was somewhat fragile when they had met in college. Even in her early 20s his young wife seemed to be the sort of person who had things go wrong, but it just didn't make sense that she had so many problems.

Things had gotten a little better since they had started working with Dr. Gardner the year before. His wife liked Dr. Gardner, a young physician in her early 30s. Dr. Gardner tried to spend time with his wife, to reassure her, to answer her questions, and to be available by phone, but the problems continued—she had so many of them. First, she had female problems. She had been diagnosed as having something called endometriosis. Her periods were always very severe. Many times she would have to stay in bed for two or three days because of the pain and cramping. She had undergone a hysterectomy two years ago because of the pain and bleeding. She also had an ovarian cyst that required surgery. Come to think of it, he didn't know any of his wife's friends who spent nearly as much time visiting doctors and being in hospitals as his wife. It seemed like she was in the hospital for something at least every year. She also had a lot of bowel problems. She was diagnosed as having colitis and irritable bowel syndrome. She had to be very careful with what she ate or she would develop belly pain and diarrhea. Her system could never get going correctly, since she usually had either diarrhea or constipation. She had been diagnosed as having fibromyalgia. She had also been diagnosed with chronic fatigue syndrome, which often left her tired and lackluster. Things had reached a point two years ago where she was seeing seven or eight different doctors for various problems. When Margaret saw Dr. Gardner and after Dr. Gardner had followed her for a while, the new doctor suggested that she coordinate his wife's care—that it wasn't always a good idea having lots of doctors involved because they didn't know what the others were doing, and it would probably be better for her to see one central person. This seemed to help in that she hadn't been hospitalized in the last year and perhaps was doing a bit better.

He still didn't understand why the doctors hadn't been able to get to the root of her problem. They had spent so much money and had so many tests done. He kept believing that there was some underlying problem that hadn't been diagnosed, as did his wife.

Their two children, Cathy, age seven, and Billy, age nine, were also suffering from the problems. For several years Margaret hadn't had the energy necessary to involve herself in school or extracurricular activities. She frequently was so tired and lethargic she couldn't play with the children at night. This left him responsible for chauffeuring the kids around and trying to keep them busy in the evening and on the weekends. He was also worried about the money. They had good insurance but now frequently there were co-pays and some things weren't covered. Also, he was worried about his advertising job. He had taken about as much time off of work as he could to help his wife manage the house and take her to doctor appointments. He was coming to the end of his rope.

II

Riding along with her husband to Dr. Gardner's office, Margaret's mind wandered from topic to topic. She thought back over all the doctors and all the hospitals. She didn't like the way doctors treated her. (Why don't they listen to me?) She could remember so many times when she had been shown into a doctor's office only to be cut off after a few minutes through her story. Doctors didn't seem to take her complaints seriously. Sometimes they would just prescribe something and send her on her way. Other times they would be condescendingly reassuring. (I have no choice if I want to get well. I have to keep seeing them.)

The current visit to Dr. Gardner was precipitated by worsening of her migraines (Nothing they've given me has helped, and this last pill just makes me sleepy.), as well as symptoms of a urinary tract infection. She was quite sure she was urinating more frequently and sometimes felt a twinge of pain when urinating. She thought this was a bladder infection, or worse a kidney infection. She had several other fears she wanted to discuss with Dr. Gardner. She had seen a news program the week before on pap tests—how poorly the technicians who read them were trained and how many mistakes they made. Did she still need pap smears now that her uterus was removed? She was also very concerned about the e-coli in uncooked meat and wanted the doctor to tell her how long she had to cook meat to be totally sure that it was free of infection. She also had the lingering fear that she might have AIDS. She had been in hospitals so many times and had received so many I.V.s and had been stuck with so many needles. She recurrently feared that she had AIDS and it simply had not shown up on the last test but might show up on the next one. She needed to talk to Dr. Gardner about these things. She shivered in anticipation and fear.

Paul and Margaret drove into the professional building lot, parked the car, and took the elevator up one flight to Dr. Gardner's office. Margaret had a short wait before she was escorted into an examination room, asked to put on an examination gown, and waited for the doctor. She sat there, anxiously gazing around the room. She read Dr. Gardner's diplomas, prominently displayed on the wall over her desk. Part of the writing was in Latin and part in Greek. She wondered to herself how someone could possibly stand being a doctor working with sick people all the time. First of all it would be too scary to be exposed to all those sick people. (What would you catch? It seems like you would always be sick. Also, how could you stand working with AIDS patients or patients with other infections. Wouldn't you constantly be worrying about contracting the disease yourself?)

Dr. Gardner entered the room and reassuringly greeted Margaret. "Nice to see you again, Margaret. I'm sorry to hear that you have been having problems. Let's go through them one at a time and see what we can do."

Fifteen minutes later Dr. Gardner had listened to Margaret's complaints about her migraines (and had suggested an alternative medicine that might be tried), indicated that they would obtain a urine sample for culture to make sure she didn't have a urinary tract infection, and reassured Margaret that even though errors were occasionally made on pap tests that hers had all been completely normal prior to the hysterectomy. She had discussed with Margaret the need to thoroughly cook all meat and reassured her that the last AIDS test she had was adequate since Margaret had not engaged in any high risk behaviors.

"Margaret, you have to remember that you are the sort of person who feels physical things more than most people. Some people don't feel much pain and some people do. You are one of the people who tends to feel things physically. I think also when you are upset or depressed about something that you tend to experience it physically. Some people are just that way. However, I don't think you really are clinically depressed or have an anxiety disorder—I've screened you for both of those—I think it's just that life's problems affect you like they do us all, but you experience them more in terms of physical symptoms. I know you worry a great deal about your health. That's why I think it is important for me to see you regularly and when necessary arrange for you to work with other doctors or specialists. But I think it is best if you continue to see just one doctor to manage your care. You remember that episode a couple of years ago when you had that period of numbness and weakness in your lower legs? Remember you had trouble standing up after you had been sitting in a chair? That improved over time and the fact that you had all those tests done and that the other doctors were considering surgery on your spine suggests to me that it is really important for you to see someone who knows you well and can coordinate your care."

Margaret was only half hearing what Dr. Gardner was saying. There was something else that she wanted to bring up today, but really didn't know how. The simple fact is that one of the main sources of conflict in her marriage for many years now had been her lack of sexual interest. She just wasn't interested in having sexual intercourse with her husband. She liked touching and liked being held, but she found the actual sexual act itself uninteresting or even repulsive. This was an ongoing source of friction between her and her husband. Her husband had again become petulant and moody about her lack of interest in sex. Was this a medical problem she should discuss with Dr. Gardner?

☐ Discussion

In considering the diagnostic criteria, this individual does appear to meet criteria for somatization disorder. Her symptoms have been present since before age 30, and she clearly is not feigning symptoms but experiences them as very real. Despite the severity and complexity of her symptoms, prior evaluations have not been fruitful in uncovering clear, perhaps reversible causes of her disorder. Also, she has various pain complaints, gastrointestinal symptom complaints, as well as a pseudoneurological and sexual complaints (the weakness in her lower extremities and sexual indifference).

It is at times very difficult to differentiate somatization disorder from various anxiety disorders, as anxiety can manifest itself in physical symptoms. Also, patients with mood disorders not uncommonly will have a variety of physical complaints. Therefore it is important to assess the mood of someone with multiple physical complaints, and most important to rule out a medical causes for these complaints. Unfortunately, once a patient is thought to be a somatisizer or a "crock," many physicians tend to be dismissive of their complaints. Because of this true medical illnesses that can be severe may be overlooked.

This disorder is differentiated from hypocondriasis in that multiple organ systems and complaints are present over time. It is differentiated from body dysmorphic disorder because there does not appear to be a defect in physical appearance to the individual. Also it is not purely a pain disorder since some of the symptoms clearly do not involved only pain per se.

Somatization disorder is a chronic, often fluctuating illness that usually begins with some symptoms as early as adolescence but is clearly well established by age 30. In various studies it is found to be more common in women than men, although some of this may reflect the bias of male physicians who are more likely to label female patients as having this disorder. The nature of the somatic symptoms vary across various ethnic and cultural groups.

The course of illness for many of these patients is often difficult and at times dangerous. These individuals often see multiple physicians with various physical complaints. Early in the course of the illness, physicians may attempt to deal with these symptoms through various diagnostic procedures, pharmacotherapy, and in certain situations, surgical management. The end result is often frustrating for the physician and patient alike. Exposure to various medications and surgeries increases the likelihood that some organic problem will develop. For example, patients who have multiple abdominal surgeries are at risk of developing adhesions of the bowel that may then result in bowel obstruction.

Although the physician in this scenario deals very effectively with this patient, many physicians become frustrated by patients with somatization disorder, and, once they realize that this is the underlying problem, tend to be dismissive of them. Therefore, although these patients do best when seen regularly and reassured, physicians tend to deal with them abruptly and don't want to see them again soon.

The complications of this disorder mainly relate to the evaluation procedures and treatments to which these people are exposed. Also, because affected individuals usually involve themselves with multiple caregivers, their care is often fragmented. It is extremely useful to have one physician who is knowledgeable about such patients and competent in their management to coordinate their care, see them regularly, and involve other consultants only when necessary. If comorbid conditions such as depression or panic disorder are present, treatments for these conditions can be initiated as well, although this group of patients commonly develop side effects from pharmacotherapy.

☐ Questions for Further Discussion

1) Some physicians tend to become angry with patients who fall into this diagnostic group. Why do you think that is and how can it be avoided?
2) How should Dr. Gardner deal with Margaret's husband? What information should she provide him?

3) Since there is significant overlap, why don't we consider somatization disorder as either an anxiety disorder or a mood disorder?

☐ References

American Psychiatric Association. (1994). *Diagnostic and statistical manual of mental disorders* (4th ed.). Washington, DC: Author.

☐ Suggested Readings

Barsky, A. J., & Borus, J. F. (1999). Functional somatic syndromes. *Annuals of Internal Medicine, 130,* 910–921.

Barsky, A. J. (1998). A comprehensive approach to the chronically somatizing patient. *Journal of Psychosomatic Research, 45,* 301–306.

Epstein, R. M., Quill, T. E., & McWhinney, I. R. (1999). Somatization reconsidered: Incorporating the patient's experience of illness. *Archives of Internal Medicine, 159,* 215–222.

Ford, C. V. (1997). Somatization and fashionable diagnoses: Illness as a way of life. *Scandinavian Journal of Work, Environment & Health, 23,* 7–16.

Fritz, G. K., Fritsch, S., & Hagino, O. (1997). Somatoform disorders in children and adolescents: A review of the past 10 years. *Journal of American Academy of Child and Adolescent Psychiatry, 36,* 1329–1338.

Katon, W. J., & Walker, E. A. (1998). Medically unexplained symptoms in primary care. *Journal of Clinical Psychiatry, 59,* 5–21.

Lipowski, Z. J. (1990). Somatization and depression. *Psychosomatics, 31,* 13–21.

Mai, FM. (1995). "Hysteria" in clinical neurology. *Canadian Journal of Neurological Science, 22,* 101–110.

McWhinney, I. R., Epstein, R. M., & Freeman, T. R. (1997). Rethinking somatization. *Annuals of Internal Medicine, 126,* 747–750.

Saravay, S. M. (1996). Psychiatric interventions in the medically ill: Outcome and effectiveness research. *Psychiatric Clinics of North America, 19,* 467–480.

Singh, B. S. (1998). Managing somatoform disorders. *Medical Journal of Australia, 168,* 572–577.

Smith, G. R. (1992). The epidemiology and treatment of depression when it coexists with somatoform disorders, somatization, or pain. *General Hospital Psychiatry, 14,* 265–272.

Stuart, S., & Noyes, R. Jr. (1999). Attachment and interpersonal communication in somatization. *Psychosomatics, 40,* 334–343.

Walker, E. A. (1997). Medically unexplained physical symptoms. *Clinical Obstetrics and Gynecology, 40,* 589–600.

16

CHAPTER

Body Dysmorphic Disorder

☐ Introduction

Individuals who have body dysmorphic disorder are greatly concerned about what they perceive to be a defect in their appearance. This may be an exaggerated concern about some minor, unusual physical feature, or it may have no basis in reality at all. Often the perceived problem is in the head and neck area, although it can involve any body part. These people are very concerned about this perceived abnormality, spend a great deal of time worrying about it, and often spend much time examining the perceived defect in the mirror or asking for reassurance about it. They may seek help from physicians hoping that the condition can be corrected. Some end up undergoing plastic surgery and are usually unhappy with the result.

In considering the following scenario, remember the following points:

1) What is the pattern of onset of this disorder in this individual?
2) What have the social consequences of this disorder been for this individual?
3) Body dysmorphic disorder is sometimes difficult to separate from normal concerns about appearance. Do people's concerns about appearance vary over their lifecycle? What age group is most likely to have heightened concerns in this regard?

☐ **Diagnostic Criteria**
(DSM-IV)

A. Preoccupation with an imagined defect in appearance. If a slight physical anomaly is present, the person's concern is markedly excessive.
B. The preoccupation causes clinically significant distress or impairment in social, occupational, or other important areas of functioning.
C. The preoccupation is not better accounted for by another mental disorder (e.g., dissatisfaction with body shape and size in Anorexia Nervosa).

☐ **The Stories**

I

Jack Smiley was taken to an exam room by the nurse. As the door closed, he sat in the chair by the basin, casually picked up a *People* magazine that was lying on the floor and began to flip through it. Almost at once his left hand came up to his left cheek and began feeling the holes, or "trenches" as he sometimes called them. He glanced around the room and saw a mirror to his left. Tossing the magazine to the floor he stood and walked to the mirror. Turning one cheek then the other, he looked at his face in the mirror (God, they look horrible. I can't believe how big these holes are. It looks like somebody fired a shotgun into my face.) He had developed a ritual where he would turn one cheek, then the other, looking at the scars, counting them, and then feeling them with the tips of his fingers (God I'm ugly. I can't believe how I look.).

Jack thought back over the last few years. He was now 25, a stock broker. It looked like his career was going well at first, but now he was known as the loner. He didn't drop in on anybody else for coffee, and he wouldn't go out and have a beer after work. When his boss invited him over for dinner he always thought up an excuse. (People won't be able to eat if they have to look at my face.) He hated to meet with clients and always tried to do his business over the phone, but that only went so far. In his work he knew that sometimes you had to meet with people, talk with people, be friendly with people. It was hard for him to allow people to see him though because of his perceived ugliness.

It had reached a point where he was unable to live with it any longer. Over the objections of his wife, he had called and made appointments to again see a dermatologist and a plastic surgeon. He had seen both in the past but was told that his insurance would not pay for dermabrasion or injections, and he also was told that he really didn't have a significant problem. After leaving the office he had been somewhat reassured for a few minutes, but it didn't last, and now, although insurance wouldn't pay, he was going to go ahead and have the procedures done anyway. He couldn't stand it any longer.

His wife was very intolerant of this. She at first tried to reassure him and tell him he really had no noticeable facial scars, but he knew she wasn't being truthful with him and was just trying to hide her true feelings. In recent months she had become increasingly angry with him when she found him in front of a mirror. He had started going to the bathroom in the basement where he was less likely to be discovered. She would become frustrated and yell, "Your face is fine. It's all in your head," and had repeatedly suggested to him that he see a counselor or a psychiatrist, but he realized the problem wasn't in his head, it was on his face. He just wasn't willing to live this way any longer.

II

Dr. Sam Navello paused outside the exam door, took the chart from the plastic case on the wall, and leafed through it. (Jack Smiley again). He turned to his last note.

"Twenty-five year old male preoccupied with minor post-acne scar formation on both cheeks, hardly visible. Treatment: Reassurance. Return if needed."

He shook his head. (This is not good. He's one of those people that worries all the time about how they look. I've got to try to not upset him and maybe get him referred to a psychiatrist.)

As the door opened he greeted Jack, "Mr. Smiley, nice to see you again. How have you been?"

"Oh fine, doc. Things have been going just fine, but I wanted to see you again about my scars. People stare at me, I'm not advancing in my work because of the way they make me look. I need to do something. A dermatologist I saw a few years ago told me that dermabrasion might be a possibility but that it was expensive, would require several sessions, and wouldn't be covered by my insurance. I'm coming back to see you to request that you consider doing it. I understand it can be painful and expensive."

"Jack, I don't know exactly how to tell you this but . . . I think you worry too much about the scars on your face. Actually they are hardly even there. Most men have minor residual skin changes from acne during adolescence. Yours are really very modest compared to other people. You're actually a good looking young man. You look young and healthy, and I understand you're married and you have a good job. I think you're preoccupied with this thing. You're focusing on it and obsessing about it. I don't think its really a problem and I'm sure its not affecting the way people treat you at work. I think this is more of a psychological issue and I'd like to refer you to see a psychiatrist."

Jack was dismayed. He had heard this line before. He did not understand why people tried to humor him rather than help him.

Later after listening to more of Dr. Navello's advice and encouragement, he left the office, tossed the referral information about the psychiatrist in the trash bin by the elevator, and began to plan his schedule so that he would be able to have time for the office appointment with the plastic surgeon the next Wednesday.

☐ Discussion

Clearly Jack is very preoccupied about what he perceives to be significant facial lesions. Whether or not he has visible acne scars, they apparently are not substantial enough to cause concern to anyone in his environment. Others around him are surprised (and in the case of his wife, annoyed) at his preoccupation. Clearly this is affecting his work and his relationship with his wife, and may also eventually affect him financially. Although a complete interview would be necessary, we have no evidence that there is any other psychiatric disorder present that might explain this phenomenon.

Body dysmorphic disorder has only recently been studied in detail. The condition is also known as dysmorphophobia. We know little about the disorder in terms of prevalence rates, although what limited data are available would suggest that the disorder occurs about equally in males and females. It usually begins in adolescence or young adulthood and many times runs a waxing and waning course. Not uncommonly, people with this disorder seek some sort of medical care for what they perceive as their problem and are frequently seen in dermatologists' or plastic surgeons' offices. Often the surgical result is not positive since the perceived abnormality frequently persists.

Anorexia nervosa is also characterized by misperception of the body but in this case other symptoms make it clear that the disorder is primarily an eating disorder. Also, the somatic type of delusional disorder must be considered in the differential of someone with body dysmorphic disorder, and it can be difficult to know at times which of these two diagnoses is most appropriate. It isn't completely clear that these are separate disorders.

Little is known about the treatment of these patients although structured counseling techniques, including cognitive behavioral therapy, are at times used, as are antidepressants.

☐ Questions for Further Discussion

1) Most of us have certain body parts that we consider less attractive or desirable. Therefore, do you think body dysmorphic disorder perhaps is an extreme of what is a normal pattern?
2) Many forms psychopathology represent extremes of the "normal." Give some other examples.

☐ References

American Psychiatric Association. (1994). *Diagnostic and statistical manual of mental disorders* (4th ed.). Washington, DC: Author.

☐ Suggested Readings

Albertini, R. S., & Phillips, K. A. (1999). Thirty-three cases of body dysmorphic disorder in children and adolescents. *Journal of the American Academy of Child and Adolescent Psychiatry, 38,* 453–459.

Barsky, A. J., & Borus, J. F. (1999). Functional somatic syndromes. *Annuals of Internal Medicine, 130,* 910–921.

Cousin, G. C. (1998). Body dysmorphic disorder versus manipulative behavior. *British Journal of Oral Maxiollofacial Surgery, 36,* 479.

Hollander, E., Neville, D., Frenkel, M., Josephson, S., & Liebowitz, M. R. (1992). Body dysmorphic disorder: Diagnostic issues and related disorders. *Psychosomatics, 33,* 156–165.

Mawn, L. A., & Jordan, D. R. (1998). Dysmorphophobia: A distorted perception of one's self-appearance. *Ophthalmalogic Plastic Reconstructive Surgery, 14,* 446–450.

Phillips, K. A., Gunderson, C. G., Mallya, G., McElroy, S. L., & Carter, W. (1998). A comparison study of body dysmorphic disorder and obsessive-compulsive disorder. *Journal of Clinical Psychiatry, 59,* 568–575.

Wilhelm, S., Otto, M. W., Lohr, B., & Deckersbach, T. (1999). Cognitive behavior group therapy for body dysmorphic disorder: A case series. *Behavior Research Therapy, 37,* 71–75.

VII FACTITIOUS DISORDERS

Factitious disorder involves reporting or inducing physical and/or psychological symptoms in order to become or remain a patient and interact with the medical establishment. Factitious disorder must be differentiated from malingering in which the individual produces the symptoms with a specific goal in mind such as avoiding work or obtaining disability. In factitious disorder the goal is to be a patient, pure and simple.

CHAPTER

Factitious Disorder

☐ Introduction

Individuals with factitious disorder produce physical or psychological signs or symptoms as a means of interacting with the medical establishment, being patients, having tests done on them, and being hospitalized. While most of us don't desire the sick role and prefer to avoid doctors and hospitals when we can, individuals with this uncommon disorder constantly seek medical evaluation and treatment. Of interest, many of these people have histories of careers in the health field or close relationships with those who have such careers (e.g., wife or husband of a doctor, a former nurse). At many times they are quite sophisticated about the illnesses they portray, reading widely about their purported ailments. They seek care, and usually hospitalization, from multiple caregivers at various settings, but are not forthcoming about their histories. Occasionally, individuals with this disorder travel widely (e.g., from state to state) seeking care. There are two subtypes, one with predominantly psychological signs and symptoms (e.g., complaints of senility, memory impairment), or physical signs and symptoms (e.g., nausea and vomiting, abdominal pain, bleeding, weight loss).

In considering the following scenario, consider these issues:

1) This individual clearly wants to be in the sick role. What might motivate her to seek such a role? What purpose does it serve for her?

2) What are the health risks of having factitious disorder?
3) How much would you estimate the cost of her care to be in this scenario?

☐ Diagnostic Criteria
(DSM-IV)

A. Intentional production or feigning of physical or psychological signs or symptoms.
B. The motivation for the behavior (such as economic gain, avoiding legal responsibility, or improving physical well-being, as in Malingering) are absent.

☐ The Stories

I

Nan Worthington was the name she had given the nurse at the emergency room check-in window. She indicated that she had state medical assistance insurance, was visiting from out of town, and didn't have a local doctor. Her chief complaint was that a cut she had obtained on her left arm had gotten red and painful, and she was feverish. She thought, perhaps, that she had an infection. The nurse, whose name was Flora, gave her a clipboard with a form to fill out and asked her to take a seat opposite the desk.

She sat down and began completing the form. It asked her age (29), her address (she entered the address of an apartment in a neighboring community about two hours away), medical insurance information (she entered the number for the state medical assistance plan that was her health insurance), her chief complaint (I cut myself and now I think I have an infection), her past medical history (she indicated that she had been hospitalized for a tonsillectomy at age 12 and for an appendectomy at age 16), her allergies (she denied any, although she was allergic to penicillin), her medications (she indicated oral contraceptives), her social history (she indicated she was divorced, currently unemployed, and living with her mother), her education (she indicated she was a high school graduate, which was true, but she failed to mention that she had successfully completed two years of nursing school before being discharged from school because of interpersonal problems with her instructors and the other students). On the review of systems form she checked yes to the following symptoms: pain, fever, headache, insomnia. On a line where it asked for her physician's name she indicated "none locally." When asked who to contact in case of an emergency she entered the name of her mother at her mother's old address from several years ago (her mother didn't live there any longer). She arose from her chair, crossed the room, placed the clipboard in front of the nurse who was talking on the phone, and retreated to her chair. She would wait for a while. She was used to waiting in emergency rooms. Occasionally they took you right in; that was usually only if you were brought in by an ambulance. (For an infection they make you wait awhile. It is only after they see a bad infection that they start to take you seriously.)

Flora disappeared down the hallway only to return a few minutes later and invite Nan to accompany her to one of the examination rooms. She followed the nurse down the hall and together they turned left into a cramped examining room that featured most prominently an exam table, a long goose neck lamp, a small desk and chair, and various sundry medical supplies on shelves. Flora had her sit on the chair, took her temperature with an electronic thermometer, commenting "My, my. Your fever is 103°." Took her pulse (96 and regular at her right wrist), and then her blood pressure (104/70 right arm sitting). The nurse then sat on the edge of the exam table, placed the clipboard in front of her, reshuffled the papers, and said "Now Ms. Worthington, tell me more about why you are here. You have some kind of infection?"

Nan began, "Yes, well, I cut myself in the kitchen about a week ago. I was cutting up some vegetables and wasn't thinking. I turned funny and the knife went into my arm. I didn't think much about it. I just wrapped it up with an Ace bandage although it did bleed quite a bit. Anyway, I thought it would probably heal on its own but it didn't. Then it started to turn red and puffy and started to hurt. About two days ago I started running a fever."

Flora said, "Let's have a look." As Nan outstretched her arm, Flora gently unrolled the Ace bandage from around her lower left arm and then unrolled the gauze that was underneath. She had expected a small knife wound with a localized infection. Instead, as soon a she saw the gauze she also saw the pus from the wound, smelled the infection, and reevaluated the significance of this wound as something far worse than she had anticipated. The wound was on the under-surface of Nan's arm, was approximately six inches in length, quite deep, gaping, and clearly infected, with pus in and around the wound, redness extending for several inches on all sides of the wound, and streaks of infection extending up above her elbow to her upper arm. This was a bad infection and the patient was probably septic (meaning the infection has spread to her blood).

"Ooh, this is not good," said Flora almost involuntarily, and then gave a smile to reassure her patient and said, "I think we should have Dr. Carter look at this as soon as he is free. He's casting a broken bone right now and it'll probably just be another 15 minutes. I'm going to go ahead and draw some blood from you."

She proceeded to draw three tubes of blood from the patient's right arm and said, "I'm going to run these down to the lab and I'll be right back. Just make yourself comfortable."

Nan sat on the chair and looked at her arm. (Yep, I've done it this time. This one's a doozy). She thought about what would transpire over the next hour. She assumed the doctor wouldn't be there in 15 minutes, it would be at least a half hour (It always takes longer than they say it will.). He would look at the wound, chastise her for not having it sutured, and then chastise her again for not coming in as soon as there was evidence of an infection. He would tell her that this is serious, that the infection may have spread to her bloodstream, and that she would probably need to be hospitalized for I.V. antibiotic therapy. He might also tell her that he was calling in a surgeon to look at the wound to see if it needed debridement (or he might not), but instead admit her and figure that out later. At any rate, she knew she would be in the hospital several days and when the wound failed to respond to intravenous antibiotics (as it would fail to do because she would continue to manipulate it and contaminate it), she would probably have to stay for at least a week. There was no hurry. She sat back in the chair and casually picked up a magazine that was lying on the desk and thumbed through it.

II

Dr. Larry Johnson, a psychiatrist, received a call from Dr. Bruce Peterson about a patient named Nan.

"This is Dr. Johnson," he replied as he picked up his page on the wall phone outside the hospital cafeteria where he had just eaten lunch.

"Hi Larry, it's Bruce Peterson. How are you?"

"Fine thanks, just got back from vacation and ready to go."

"Glad to hear it," said Bruce, "because I need your help. We've got a woman up on 6B named Nan Worthington. She came in with a rather advanced bacterial infection on her forearm. It was really rather strange that she let the infection go for so long, and she was septic when she came in. Have you got time to hear about this now?"

"Sure," said Larry, "go ahead."

"Well at first things seemed to go along fine. She was pleasant and cooperative and the nurses had no problem with her. We started her on I.V. antibiotics and I assumed the infection would start to clear in 24 to 48 hours. However, it didn't. When the culture and sensitivity report came back it looked like the wound had been contaminated with oral and rectal flora. I think she's contaminating the wound with her own spit and feces. The nurses have noticed that the bandage on the wound has been taken off and put back on when they haven't changed it, and then last night on rounds they told me that they had seen the patient disconnect her I.V. and run the antibiotic into the sink. I'm thinking she's one of those people who make themselves sick."

"Factitious disorder," said Larry.

"Yeah. Would you mind stopping by to see her?"

"Sure, I'll be glad to, but you should alert her to the fact that I'm coming. I wouldn't be surprised if she refuses to talk to me and may sign out of the hospital."

☐ Discussion

These stories suggest that this individual is producing this physical problem herself and we have no evidence that there is some particular incentive such as disability payments that would be motivating her behavior. In the DSM-IV this would be classified as "with predominantly physical signs and symptoms" as opposed to "with predominantly psychological signs and symptoms" or "mixed."

Despite the fact that these cases are fairly commonly seen in medical settings, many go unidentified. We know very little about the prevalence of this condition, although there is suggestion in the literature that this disorder is more common in men then women. One of the problems in ascertaining prevalence is the fact that these patients may be reported by physicians at various facilities under different names over time. Therefore one individual may account for many cases. As far as can be ascertained, this disorder tends to be chronic and recurrent and these individuals rarely seek psychiatric care.

The goal of therapy is in some way to restrict these individual's access to care so that their healthcare can be managed by a single provider who can monitor their behavior and insure that expensive, and potentially dangerous, medical evaluation and treatment procedures are not undertaken unless clearly indicated.

☐ Questions for Further Discussion

1) What symptoms might someone feign if they were presenting with predominantly psychological signs and symptoms?

2) Americans are very protective of their medical records, and records cannot be released from one facility to another or from one health care provider to another without the patient's written permission. However, were a national standardized database of patients to be established, it would be relatively easy to identify individuals with factitious disorder and refer them for psychiatric care. What are the arguments for or against setting up such a database?

☐ References

American Psychiatric Association. (1994). *Diagnostic and statistical manual of mental disorders* (4th ed.). Washington, DC: Author.

☐ Suggested Readings

Joe, E. K., Li, V. W., Magro, C. M., Arndt, K. A., & Bowers, K. E. (1999). Diagnostic clues to dermatitis artefacta. *Cutis, 63,* 209–214.

O'Hara, M. (1998). Cracking the crock: How to deal with factitious eye disease. *Journal of Ophthalmic Nursing and Technology, 17,* 188–192.

Louis, D. S., & Jebson, P. J. (1998). Mimickers of hand infections. *Hand Clinics, 14,* 519–529.

Robertson, M. M., & Cervilla, J. A. (1997). Munchausen's syndrome. *British Journal of Hospital Medicine, 58,* 308–312.

McKane, J. P., & Anderson, J. (1997). Munchausen's syndrome: Rule breakers and risk takers. *British Journal of Hospital Medicine, 58,* 150–153.

Mydo, J. H., Macchia, R. J., & Kanter, J. L. (1997). Munchausen's syndrome: A medicolegal dilemma. *Medical and Science Law, 37,* 198–201.

Murray, J. B. (1997). Munchausen syndrome/Munchausen syndrome by proxy. *Journal of Psychology, 131,* 343–362.

Lande, R. G. (1996). Factitious disorders and the "professional patient." *Journal of the American Osteopath Association, 96,* 468–472.

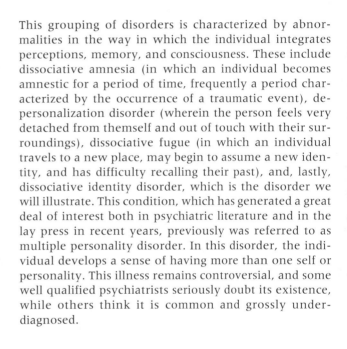

PART

VIII DISSOCIATIVE DISORDERS

This grouping of disorders is characterized by abnormalities in the way in which the individual integrates perceptions, memory, and consciousness. These include dissociative amnesia (in which an individual becomes amnestic for a period of time, frequently a period characterized by the occurrence of a traumatic event), depersonalization disorder (wherein the person feels very detached from themselves and out of touch with their surroundings), dissociative fugue (in which an individual travels to a new place, may begin to assume a new identity, and has difficulty recalling their past), and, lastly, dissociative identity disorder, which is the disorder we will illustrate. This condition, which has generated a great deal of interest both in psychiatric literature and in the lay press in recent years, previously was referred to as multiple personality disorder. In this disorder, the individual develops a sense of having more than one self or personality. This illness remains controversial, and some well qualified psychiatrists seriously doubt its existence, while others think it is common and grossly underdiagnosed.

Dissociative Identity Disorder

☐ Introduction

Dissociative identity disorder is characterized by two or more personalities that periodically exert control over the individual. Although certain personalities may be aware of other ones, there is amnesia for some events by one or more of the personalities. Personalities can vary a great deal in terms of their characteristics and traits, and many times are at considerable variance from other personalities. There is often a primary or central identity, and the individual identities may have different names, ages, and opinions. Although most individuals have ten or fewer identities, individuals with more than 100 have been reported. In reviewing the following scenarios, consider the following:

1) How would you contrast the two personalities illustrated in this scenario? What traits and proclivities characterize each personality?
2) In each story there is a shift from one personality to another. What are the triggers, and why might these be important?

☐ Diagnostic Criteria
(DSM-IV)

A. The presence of two or more distinct identities or personality states (each with its own relatively enduring pattern of perceiving, relating to, and thinking about the environment and self).

B. At least two of these identities or personality states recurrently take control of the person's behavior.
C. Inability to recall important personal information that is too extensive to be explained by ordinary forgetfulness.
D. The disturbance is not due to the direct physiological effects of a substance (e.g., blackouts or chaotic behavior during Alcohol Intoxication) or a general medical condition (e.g., complex partial seizures). **Note**: In children, the symptoms are not attributable to imaginary playmates or other fantasy play.

☐ The Stories

I

Jill Harmon was sitting in her apartment eating dinner (leftovers as usual) and watching the news. She was curled up in the brown leather chair opposite the television. She was most interested in the weather, which would be coming up in a few minutes, since she had plans to be outdoors the next afternoon. She didn't really like the news. First was this dumb story about a new sports facility being built in town, then a special feature on traffic accidents. Now the camera cut to a reporter on the street outside of a housing project. Jill stared at the television transfixed. The rape and murder of an adolescent girl had occurred earlier that afternoon. There were no suspects as of yet. The brutality of the crime was hideous. Jill was shocked and dismayed and felt an old feeling coming back, and before she could do anything about it, Susie had taken over.

Susie knew all about Jill. Jill was the good one, the nice one, the positive one, the sucker, the stupid one who didn't realize the way the world really was, but Susie knew the world. Susie knew its blackness. She knew the way things really were. She knew about men. Men always wanted violent sex. It was a sick, sick world and she wanted nothing to do with it. When she got mad, and boy she got mad, she would throw things. What the hell? And she would cut. Cutting was one of the things that allowed her to relax and calm down. She thought of the whole procedure: going to the grocery store, buying the razor blades, going home, locking the door, lighting a candle, sitting in the big leather chair. It wasn't painful, it didn't hurt. The important thing was the blood. She liked to see the blood as it seeped out of the wound and ran down her arm. This had been a bad day and she needed to relax.

The weatherman was on the television predicting showers for to-morrow. (What else is new? I knew it would rain. Those guys are always wrong anyway. What the hell.) She took the plastic container, now empty of food, and threw it into the kitchen. She uncurled her legs and walked into the bathroom. She had a new pack of razors. She liked them when they were brand new; they were shaper and clean. She selected the top one, returned to the living room, lit the candle on the table to her left with the box of matches, and curled up in the big leather chair. She picked up the remote and turned off the T.V. She turned to her right and turned on the radio. No, she wanted it quiet tonight, and turned it back off. She then extended her left arm, underside up and holding the razor in her right hand made a transverse cut halfway up her forearm. It didn't hurt. At first there was nothing but a thin red line, and then the blood started to well up out of it and as she raised her arm the blood formed a long, slowly moving rivulet down her arm toward her elbow. She was pleased and relaxed.

II

Janet Page, who had been an E.R. nurse at the county hospital in Des Moines, Iowa for nearly 25 years, enjoyed her work but found the increasing violence in the city concerning, and the cases brought in that resulted from that violence increasingly difficult to manage. When an ambulance driver arrived at the E.R. desk and said he had brought in a young woman who had tried to kill herself, Janet, as nursing supervisor, told the other two nurses at the station that she would admit the girl to the emergency room, and see what sort of help she needed. The ambulance driver said the girl had cut her wrists and arms, a phenomenon Janet had seen all too many times, but never could quite understand.

She knocked quietly on the door and entered the room. The girl was slight, with long dark hair that needed a good washing. She was sitting in the corner by the sink, in blue jeans, running shoes, and a T-shirt, with her legs pulled up into her chest, gently rocking. She glanced up with a sorrowful look in her eyes as Janet walked in and sat down in the chair opposite her. She knew she shouldn't rush things (. . . just be patient). After sitting there for a few moments she said, "Hi, I'm Janet. I'm the head nurse here. I wanted to come by and see what happened and what we need to do to help you. How are you doing?"

In a quiet tentative voice the girl replied, "Fine, I think."

Janet said, "What's your name?"

The girl replied, "Jill Harmon."

"How old are you?"

"Nineteen," although she looked younger to Janet. The girl seemed shy, inhibited, and probably depressed. Janet quickly perused the situation from a medical standpoint. Although the girl looked frail, she clearly was not near exsanguination. The ambulance team had put bandages on both arms and very little blood had soaked through. The girl had good coloring, and she judged that she had time to talk to the girl a bit longer before being intrusive about the wounds. However, she did need to check the girl's blood pressure and pulse.

"I'm just going to check your vital signs to make sure things are okay."

The girl extended her left arm as Janet placed the cuff above the elbow.

"You must have had a pretty rough day," volunteered Janet as the girl continued to gaze distantly in front of her, eyes focused vaguely somewhere in the far corner. "Want to tell me about it?"

"This is going to sound weird, but I really don't remember what happened. I remember being really upset, and the next thing I knew the ambulance was at my apartment. This happens to me sometimes. I just don't realize what's happened."

"Have you hit your head or anything, or fallen?"

"No," replied the girl.

"Do you use any drugs or medications?"

"No. I smoked pot a few times but I really didn't like it."

"Have you been having thoughts about harming yourself or killing yourself?"

"No, not at all. That's what's really weird about this. I've actually been feeling pretty good. Things are going okay. I have a new part time job lined up as a waitress and things are going okay for me, I guess."

"Do you live alone?"

"Yeah, I have an apartment over by the university."

"Are you a student?" asked Janet.

"I was in school for a while but it didn't seem to work out. I just couldn't seem to concentrate and get things done. I kept forgetting things, like this. It's really weird."

Janet now began to take off the dressings and carefully examine the girls arms. This clearly was not the first time she had lacerated her forearms. She had evidence of extensive scarring on both arms as high as the elbow. The pattern was very extensive and suggested that the girl had carved on herself many times before.

"Have you been depressed, or are you under psychiatric care?" asked Janet.

"I saw a counselor a few times when I was in high school, but it really didn't help. Also, they had a psychiatrist see me a couple of times in the emergency room, but that never worked out either."

"Do you have any close friends who could give you support or help?"

"I have a friend, Julie, but she moved away last summer. I really don't have any close friends now." Then she added, "I had a boyfriend a few months ago but he turned out to be really weird, into drugs. I thought I was really in love with him but it didn't work out. It all happened so fast."

Janet asked, "Do you have a boyfriend now?"

The girl replied, "No. I generally don't like guys. See, my father used to bother me . . . I mean sexually, when I was a kid and I'm weird about sex and men. I think they are going to take advantage of me."

Janet found this sudden revelation disquieting.

"Well look, I think it would be a good idea if I brought the doctor in to see you. His name is Dr. Navarre. He's a nice guy. We need him to look at your arms and see if they need sutures. Do you think you're okay to talk to him now?"

"Sure. I'll be fine."

As Janet reached the door she turned back. The girl looked so small and waif-like in the corner. Janet reached the nursing desk and cornered Dr. Navarre, who was charting. She filled him in on the information she had and suggested that it would be good for him to look at the arms. She had planned to go back in with him but was called away by one of the other nurses to help start an I.V. Dr. Schmidt entered the room alone. Janet then became involved in helping another nurse get ready to put a chest tube into a trauma victim in the next room. She got involved in what she was doing and was very surprised when the door Dr. Navarre had gone through ten minutes earlier flew open and he stomped out. The sphygmomanometer and stethoscope, evidently thrown by the girl inside, struck him on the back. She heard a woman scream, "You asshole! Get the hell out of here!" The voice was shrill and nasty. Dr. Navarre turned around as Janet approached, "I couldn't believe it. I thought you said she was quiet and shy. She was angry with me as soon as I walked in the door. I've never had a patient call me such horrible names. She was up and pacing and yelling profanities, and when I finally asked her if I could look at her wrists she yelled no and started throwing things. I think she's crazy."

Janet was quite perplexed. How could this have happened?

☐ Discussion

In this scenario we have evidence of two distinct identities that have taken control of the individual's behavior at different times. We have evidence that personal information cannot be recalled (Jill doesn't remember what happened prior to coming to the emergency room), and we have no evidence that the problem is secondary to drug use or a medical condition.

Dissociative identity disorder is quite controversial. A number of clinicians and researchers believe that this is a common, frequently overlooked problem. Others are highly doubtful that it even exists, or that if it does it is probably engendered during psychotherapy delivered to some patients who are encouraged to see problems as separate "parts" of themselves.

Literature suggests that individuals with this disorder have a high rate of prior physical and sexual abuse, particularly during childhood. Self-mutilation and other impulse control problems are often evident. Comorbidity for certain diagnostic groupings including borderline personality disorder are quite common. The disorder is far more common in females than males. Many of the cases that have been reported have occurred in the United States, and it is unclear whether there might be some cultural bias. The disorder usually runs a chronic, recurrent course. Adequate data on a possible hereditary component is not available.

The treatment of dissociative identity disorder is usually presumed to be insight-oriented psychotherapy, although very little formal empirical treatment research on this disorder has been conducted.

☐ Questions for Further Discussion

1) What are your thoughts about dissociative identity disorder? Do you believe it exists?
2) People clearly do have different levels of consciousness, for example, when we sleep. Another example would be when we're driving somewhere and suddenly realize that we have not been paying attention to what we were doing; we have been operating the car, just not consciously. Do such alternative states suggest to you the possibility of dissociative identity disorder?

☐ References

American Psychiatric Association. (1994). *Diagnostic and statistical manual of mental disorders* (4th ed.). Washington, DC: Author.

☐ Suggested Readings

Atchison, M., & McFarlane, A. C. (1994). A review of dissociation and dissociative disorders. *Australian and New Zealand Journal of Psychiatry, 28,* 591–599.

Behnke, S. H. (1997). Confusion in the courtroom. How judges have assessed the criminal responsibility of individuals with multiple personality disorder. *International Journal of Law Psychiatry, 20,* 293–310.

Brenner, I. (1996). The characterological basis of multiple personality. *American Journal of Psychotherapy, 50,* 154–166.

Coons, P. M. (1998). The dissociative disorders. Rarely considered and underdiagnosed. *Psychiatric Clinics of North America, 21,* 637–648.

Frankel, F. H. (1996). Dissociation: The clinical realities. *American Journal of Psychiatry, 13,* 64–70.

McDowell, D. M., Levine, F. R., & Nunes, E. V. (1999). Dissociative identity disorder and substance abuse: The forgotten relationship. *Journal of Psychoactive Drugs, 31,* 71–83.

Merskey, H., & Piper, A. Jr. (1998). Treatment of dissociative identity disorder. *American Journal of Psychiatry, 155,* 1462–1463.

Middleton, W., & Butler, J. (1998). Dissociative identity disorder: An Australian series. *Australian and New Zealand Journal of Psychiatry, 32,* 794–804.

Pope, H. G. Jr., Oliva, P. S., Hudson, J. I., Bodkin, J. A., & Gruber, A. J. (1999). Attitudes toward DSM-IV dissociative disorders diagnoses among board-certified American psychiatrists. *American Journal of Psychiatry, 156,* 321–323.

Powell, R. A., & Howell, A. J. (1998). Effectiveness of treatment for dissociative identity disorder. *Psychological Reports, 83,* 483–490.

Rifkin, A., Ghisalbert, D., Dimatou, S., Jin, C., & Sethi, M. (1998). Dissociative identity disorder in psychiatric inpatients. *American Journal of Psychiatry, 155,* 844–845.

Salama, A. A. (1995). Multiple personality disorder. *Journal of the Medical Association of Georgia, 84,* 75–79.

IX EATING DISORDERS

This section on eating disorders focuses on two primary disorders: anorexia nervosa characterized by marked weight loss and body image disturbance, and bulimia nervosa, characterized by marked concern about weight and shape issues and also by binge eating accompanied by compensatory behaviors such as self-induced vomiting.

Anorexia nervosa has been known in the medical literature for more than 100 years and has been a focus of research for much of this time. Bulimia nervosa was first described as a distinct diagnostic entity only in 1979, but has received fairly intensive examination since that time. The third grouping in the area of eating disorders is "eating disorders not otherwise specified" (EDNOS). Several examples of EDNOS are included in the DSM-IV. One which was seriously considered for inclusion as a separate diagnostic entity, binge eating disorder (BED), is not illustrated here. However, BED has been the focus of considerable research in the last decade as well. This disorder is characterized by binge eating without compensatory behaviors. BED occurs in a significant subset of those who are overweight. In particular the presence of binge eating seems to correlate with early onset obesity, more severe obesity, and to some extent with the presence of other comorbid psychopathology, particularly depression.

CHAPTER

Anorexia Nervosa

☐ Introduction

Anorexia nervosa is an eating disorder characterized by low body weight achieved through dieting or by a lack of weight gain during development to a point where there is evidence of physical dysfunction. Anorexia nervosa is also characterized by an extreme fear of gaining weight (which often worsens as the individual loses weight), and misperception of one's own body (feeling fat although being thin, or at least failing to appreciate the seriousness of the low body weight). Amenorrhea, which is an easily ascertainable index of significant starvation, is also present in women with anorexia nervosa.

In the following scenarios, consider the following issues:

1) Many patients with anorexia nervosa have ideas or beliefs that are quite odd and one might say approach psychotic proportion, but they all relate to food, eating, and weight. What are the strange ideas this young woman developed?
2) What would it be like to be the parent of an adolescent or young adult with anorexia nervosa? How would it affect the family?
3) What are the specific eating disorder behaviors in which this patient engages (e.g., excessive exercise)?
4) How has having anorexia nervosa affected this young woman psychologically?

☐ Diagnostic Criteria
(DSM-IV)

A. Refusal to maintain body weight at or above a minimally normal weight for age and height (e.g., weight loss leading to maintenance of body weight less than 85% of that expected; or failure to make expected weight gain during period of growth, leading to body weight less than 85% of that expected).

B. Intense fear of gaining weight or becoming fat, even though underweight.

C. Disturbance in the way in which one's body weight or shape is experienced, undue influence of body weight or shape on self-evaluation, or denial of the seriousness of the current low body weight.

D. In postmenarcheal females, amenorrhea, i.e., the absence of at least three consecutive menstrual cycles. (A woman is considered to have amenorrhea if her periods occur only following hormone, e.g., estrogen administration).

☐ The Stories

I

Jack and Cathy Meyer were not surprised when they both received calls at work from the counselor at the high school where Sally, their 17-year-old daughter, was a junior. They knew that Sally had been having problems, and they had been encouraging her to seek help. They were worried sick about their daughter, but did not know what to do. They both agreed to come in and meet the next day with the counselor, Larry Batesman, an amiable, professorish fellow who was well liked by the students for his support and encouragement. There was a small fraction of students who disliked him for his sternness, and for the fact that he could not be manipulated when discipline was indicated.

Larry greeted Jack and Cathy warmly as he showed them into his office. (I really feel sorry for these people.) He was struck by the fact that both seemed very concerned, as one might expect, but also exhausted. He had known this family for three years and had never seen either Cathy or Jack looking so distraught.

He wasted no time in getting to the heart of the matter. "Thanks for coming in. I'm very worried about Sally. I'm sure you know I've been meeting with her every week now for the last month or so, and I don't think she's getting any better. I've been very worried about her weight. Again, as you know, she has been very thin now for about six months. We now have the school nurse weigh her on a weekly basis, and her weight is down another five pounds over the last month. I've talked with her teachers, in particular Jim Howell who, as you know, is her English teacher. He has a good relationship with her, and he is very concerned about her as well. He says she seems lethargic, disinterested, depressed. She used to be his best student. Now it's like she's not really there. Something has got to be done."

Cathy Meyer was near tears, so Jack took the lead. His anguish was apparent in his face and in his words. "We know. We've been worried sick. We talk with her every day. We've tried everything. We've told her that if she won't eat we'll force her to eat, but we can't really do that. We've told her she can't get up from the table until she eats, but she's willing to sit there all night. We've told her that we're going to put her in a hospital, but she says she won't go and runs to her room. We told her we're afraid she's going to die, and she seems unconcerned."

"How did this thing start?" asked Larry Batesman.

Cathy was now feeling in better control. "We really don't know. We noticed she was losing weight about six months ago, shortly before the Christmas holiday. She had always been a healthy, happy kid. She never really had a problem with being overweight but she's always worried about her weight. She has always talked about her weight. I can remember back when she was 14 she told me one night that she felt very uncomfortable with the fact that her body was changing, which I thought was normal, but now I wonder. She bought her own bathroom scale a few years ago and kept it in her room. Over the holidays I overheard a conversation on the phone she had with Janet Sullivan, whom you know as well. They were talking about boys, and I heard Sally say that she was sure no one would want to date her because she was so fat. She's not fat. She's never been fat, and now she is so skinny."

Jack added, "I first got worried last November, remember? She decided to be a vegetarian. I think that's when this whole thing started. She's always been a kid who worried a lot about eating red meat, but then she gave up chicken and fish, and since then the things she'll eat are almost nonexistent. She never eats with the family anymore. A few months ago she would occasionally share a meal with us if we forced it, but not since. She says she eats, but I haven't seen it. When she gets home after school she says she ate with a friend at McDonalds's, but I don't believe her. We took her to see our GP in March, thinking there might be something physically wrong, but she couldn't find anything.

She said she was thin but healthy and told her that she needed to start eating more or she would start having anemia. That didn't do any good either."

Cathy said, "And she is so unhappy. She never smiles anymore. She is in her room or—and I know this is going to sound really weird—she cooks for us. She'll never eat it, you realize, but she likes to cook elaborate meals for the rest of the family. I mean elaborate, the sort of stuff I could never fix. I have a bunch of cookbooks that I never use and she has been through most of them. Of course we encouraged the cooking, thinking she would eat some of it if she prepared the food, but that was a pipe dream."

Larry Batesman asked, "How's Rusty doing?" Rusty was Sally's 14-year-old brother. A happy, athletic kid who was well liked by his teachers.

Jack replied, "He's doing fine, but he's worried about her as well. He kids her about being a scarecrow, which makes her mad. But they've always fought—like brothers and sisters do. Lately I think he's pulled away from her. It's hard for anybody to be close to her now. She says so little, and she seems to avoid us in any kind of social situation. If we're going to a movie with Rusty, she'll turn us down. She will say she has homework. If we're going out for a meal she'll never go."

Cathy again, "We've started telling her she needs to get help, professional help. We think it's anorexia nervosa. We've gotten some books on anorexia and talked to our family doctor about it. She said it could be anorexia nervosa and she has recommended the name of a psychiatrist who can evaluate Sally. For the last two weeks we've been pushing her to go, and she's been refusing."

Larry Batesman leaned forward in his chair, "Something has to be done. I think you're going to have to make the appointment, put her in the car, take her there, and walk her in the door. I don't think you have any choice."

Cathy replied, again near tears, "I think she'll hate us forever. She gets so angry."

Jack responded, "We have no choice. I'm afraid she's going to die otherwise."

II

Sally finally got out of bed about 5:30 a.m. She had been awake off and on for two hours, and thought that maybe she could sleep a bit more now, but she always needed to get up by 5:30 to be able to get 90 minutes of exercise in before her parents awakened, and she had to get ready for school. When she was younger she had been something of a long sleeper, but not now. Although she realized she probably needed more rest, not sleeping allowed her to have the time to get everything done that she needed to do.

She pursued her usual routine. First, to work on her stomach. Her stomach had always been a big problem. Despite what she did there was always that bulge. She saw it through her clothes and she knew everyone else saw it as well. If she could just get rid of the stomach. The routine involved exactly 300 sit-ups, and she laid down at the foot of her bed and started to count them off in her head. Next for the fat burning part of the routine. She slipped out her door and down the stairs to the basement, where her father kept his exercise bike. She was on it and going. It wasn't enough to ride fast—she had to ride absolutely as fast as she could. At times her legs would cramp and she would have to stop for a moment, but as soon as that passed she was back pumping. No headphones, no T.V.; her eyes were closed and she was pumping as hard as she could, thinking of the calories that she was burning. In particular she was thinking of that extra piece of toast yesterday. She could have kicked herself for eating it. She was so hungry, and she had just eaten it impulsively. Afterwards she knew it had been wrong. She hated herself for it. (You don't break the rules. The only way this thing works is if you do it right every day. Control.)

It was almost 7:00 and she was up in her bedroom preparing to shower, but first the scale. She slipped out of her robe. First she checked to make sure that the scale was properly placed on the floor, within the marks she had drawn on the tile. If the scale had moved it might not be accurate and sometimes it scooted a bit when she got on or off. She was sure she had gained at least a pound because of the bread. She had to know but she was very frightened to find out. She was already evolving strategies in her head to work on that pound by cutting back on her intake that day. But the scale indicated that she weighed exactly the same as she had when she last weighed herself at 10:00 p.m. the night before: 87 pounds. (Okay. But I can't let it happen again.) She turned and looked at the back of the bathroom door where there was a full length mirror, mainly covered with the bathrobe. She didn't like to look at herself in the mirror, and kept the medicine cabinet open when she was brushing her teeth and flossing so that she wouldn't have to see herself, but once a day she had to check. She took down her bathrobe and laid it on top of the toilet. The routine dictated that she look at herself in the front and then at both sides. She was 5 feet 5 inches tall. The check in front was mainly to look to make sure that her legs didn't touch—in particular her thighs—when her knees were together. She could see a space there, but it was very small and she realized she would need to be constantly vigilant. The other thing to pay particular attention to was the place where her thighs flared on the sides of her legs at her hips. This area now looked fairly smooth but she was still struck overall by the flabbiness and the lack of tone in her thighs. (I don't know what to do about my thighs. I'd like to cut them open and pull out all that fat.)

Next it was the right side view and then the left. The bulge. Always the bulge projecting beyond her anterior pelvic bone. (Sloppy, flabby. I look like I'm pregnant.) Lastly, she looked at herself overall. Yes, she looked a bit tired and her upper arms did look a bit thin, but still she saw herself as too fat, and wondered if she would ever achieve the body that she wanted.

After showering and hurriedly dressing—loose fitting gym pants and a bulky, oversized sweater to hide her stomach and thighs (but people can see anyway)—she slipped back down the stairs and into the kitchen and began to prepare breakfast for the family. First, her own breakfast. A half of a piece of nine grain bread with the crust cut off, and two inches of orange juice in the glass she always used and had marked. She used to take vitamin pills, but decided not to since one of her friends told her they caused you to gain weight. She wanted to eat more, but knew that she couldn't; she felt good about her control, and felt in charge. She opened her backpack, took out the bottle of Dexatrim that she kept in the front pocket, poured five into her hand, and took them with two inches of water. (You have to watch how much water you drink or you retain fluid and look fat and sloppy. It was best to always be a little bit thirsty because that meant that you weren't looking like you were water logged.)

She began to cook eggs for her father and prepare the cereal for her mother and brother. She put on the coffee pot, poured grapefruit juice for her dad, orange juice for her mom, and apple juice for her brother, and set out the place settings. In slicing the banana to place on the cereal, she had to be very careful to keep her left hand on the peel and not actually touch the pulp, since she knew that people could absorb calories through their skin. She thought that it would be best to wear rubber gloves when preparing breakfast, but knew that her family would be upset by this, so instead she exercised great care when preparing food. Cooking the eggs was the worst part because of the constant risk that she would somehow come into direct contact with the eggs. She enjoyed cooking—was the person most likely to cook family meals—and she liked to see her family eating. It just proved what great control she had over her own body and her own needs. (Let them eat. Let them get fat if they want, I'm in control.) She then remembered the piece of bread from the day before and a sense of guilt washed over her as she started getting her things ready for school.

☐ Discussion

Sally's body weight is quite low for her age and height. The normal body weight for someone of this height would be somewhere between 110 and 140 pounds. Her weight of 87 pounds indicates she meets criteria for her weight being 85% of what would be her normal weight for height. She clearly is preoccupied with weight and shape. She demonstrates pathological eating behaviors and thinks that she is fat even though she is thin. Amenorrhea is not mentioned but we can presume that it is present.

Anorexia nervosa is a relatively common disorder among female adolescents and young adults. The mean age of onset is 17 and a full blown disorder develops in about .5% of girls and women as they traverse this period of life. Some of the other points illustrated in this scenario include the love of cooking for others (not oneself) that is sometimes seen. Also, the psychological sequellae (depression and lack of energy) are common. The majority of patients with anorexia nervosa also will meet criteria for major depressive disorder at some time. Patients with anorexia nervosa also have many obsessive-compulsive features. There have been some interesting suggestions of increased rates of obsessive-compulsive disorder and obsessive-compulsive personality disorder in first degree relatives of patients with anorexia nervosa. Generally, as people with this disorder lose weight and become thinner the obsessions and compulsions become worse. In addition to comorbidity with depression and obsessive-compulsive symptoms, many patients with anorexia nervosa will also have an anxiety disorders particularly social phobia. The longitudinal course of this disorder is highly variable but overall is often problematic with many patients remaining symptomatic for years even if they do eventually recover. Overall, the long-term mortality rate from anorexia nervosa is substantial—higher than any other psychiatric disorder—with from 5 to 15% of patients eventually dying of the disorder (two thirds from starvation, one third by suicide).

In the differential diagnosis one must certainly examine other possible reasons for weight loss. However, most individuals who lose weight for other reasons, such as those with serious medical illnesses, desire weight gain and do not have a distorted body image but instead see themselves as quite thin. Distorted body images are peculiar to anorexia nervosa patients and constitute part of the illness. Although eating disorders are usually regarded as highly culturally bound (occurring primarily in western industrialized societies where a high valence is placed on slimness as a model of attractiveness and where food is readily available, although recent evidence suggests increased rates in Third World countries), there is also strong evidence of a genetic component, since eating disorders cluster in families, and there is a higher rate of concordance among monozygotic versus dizygotic twins.

The treatment of anorexia nervosa is usually multifactorial. Not uncommonly patients will require hospitalization or partial hospital treatment during the early phase of their illness. Fairly intensive outpatient psychotherapy is also indicated. Family therapy is of particular benefit for those who have an early onset or are still living at home. Most recently, antidepressant medications, including the serotonin reuptake inhibitors have been shown to be useful in preventing relapse in weight restored patients with anorexia nervosa, although such drugs are probably not of much utility in patients who are acutely ill with the disorder and of very low weight.

☐ Questions for Further Discussion

1) Anorexia nervosa appears to be increasing in prevalence in the third world. Why would this be?
2) What are some of the medical complications of anorexia nervosa?

☐ References

American Psychiatric Association. (1994). *Diagnostic and statistical manual of mental disorders* (4th ed.). Washington, DC: Author.

☐ Suggested Readings

Andersen, A. E., & Holman, J. E. (1997). Males with eating disorders: Challenges for treatment and research. *Psychopharmacology Bulletin, 33,* 391–397.

Becker, A. E., Grinspoon, S. K., Klibanski, A., & Herzog, D. B. (1999). Eating disorders. *New England Journal of Medicine, 340,* 1092–1098.

Bowers, W. A., & Andresen, A. E. (1994). Inpatient treatment of anorexia nervosa: Review and recommendations. *Harvard Review of Psychiatry, 2,* 193–203.

Casper, R. C. (1998). Depression and eating disorders. *Depression and Anxiety, 8,* 96–104.

Casper, R. C. (1998). Recognizing eating disorders in women. *Psychopharmacology Bulletin, 34,* 267–269.

Fairburn, C. G., Shafran, R., & Cooper, Z. (1999). A cognitive behavioral theory of anorexia nervosa. *Behavior Research Therapy, 37,* 1–13.

Gilchrist, P. N., Ben-Tovim, D. I., Hay, P. J., Kalucy, R. S., & Walker, M. K. (1998). Eating disorders revisited. I: Anorexia nervosa. *Medical Journal of Australia, 169,* 438–441.

Gorwood, P., Bouvard, M., Mouren-Simeoni, M. C., Kipman, A., & Ades, J. (1998). Genetics and anorexia nervosa: A review of candidate genes. *Psychiatric Genetics, 8,* 1–12.

Herzog, D. B., Nussbaum, K. M., & Marmor, A. K. (1996). Comorbidity and outcome in eating disorders. *Psychiatric Clinics of North America, 19,* 843–859.

Jarry, J. L. (1998). The meaning of body image for women with eating disorders. *Canadian Journal of Psychiatry, 43,* 367–374.

Jeejeebhoy, K. N. (1998). Nutritional management of anorexia. *Seminars in Gastrointestinal Disease, 9,* 183–188.

Kaye, W. H., Gendall, K., & Kye, C. (1998). The role of the central nervous system in the psychoneuroendocrine disturbances of anorexia and bulimia nervosa. *Psychiatric Clinics of North America, 21,* 381–396.

Mayer, L. E., & Walsh, B. T. (1998). The use of selective serotonin reuptake inhibitors in eating disorders. *Journal of Clinical Psychiatry, 59,* 28–34.

Milosevic, A. (1999). Eating disorders and the dentist. *British Dental Journal, 186,* 109–113.

Mitchell, J. E., Crow, S., Peterson, C. B., Wonderlich, S., & Crosby, R. D. (1998). Feeding laboratory studies in patients with eating disorders: A review. *International Journal of Eating Disorders, 24,* 115–124.

Pike, K. M. (1998). Long-term course of anorexia nervosa: Response, relapse, remission, and recovery. *Clinical Psychology Review, 18,* 447–475.

Powers, P. S. (1999). Osteoporosis and eating disorders. *Journal of Pediatric and Adolescent Gynecology, 12,* 51–57.

Robin, A. L., Gilroy, M., & Dennis, A. B. (1998). Treatment of eating disorders in children and adolescents. *Clinical Psychology Review, 18,* 421–426.

Sokol, M. S., Steinberg, D., & Zerbe, K. J. (1998). Childhood eating disorders. *Current Opinion in Pediatrics, 10,* 369–377.

Steiner, H., & Lock, J. (1998). Anorexia nervosa and bulimia nervosa in children and adolescents: A review of the past 10 years. *Journal of American Academy of Child and Adolescent Psychiatry, 37,* 352–359.

Sunday, S. R., & Halmi, K. A. (1997). Eating behavior and eating disorders: The interface between clinical research and clinical practice. *Psychopharmacology Bulletin, 33,* 373–379.

Walsh, B. T., & Devlin, M. J. (1998). Eating disorders: Progress and problems. *Science, 280,* 1387–1390.

Walsh, B. T., & Kahn, C. B. (1997). Diagnostic criteria for eating disorders: Current concerns and future directions. *Psychopharmacology Bulletin, 33,* 369–372.

Wilhelm, K. A., & Clarke, S. D. (1998). Eating disorders from a primary care perspective. *Medical Journal of Australia, 168,* 458–463.

Wiseman, C. V., Harris, W. A., & Halmi, K. A. (1998). Eating disorders. *Medical Clinics of North America, 82,* 145–159.

Wolfe, B. E., Metzger, E., & Jimerson, D. C. (1997). Research update on serotonin function in bulimia nervosa and anorexia nervosa. *Psychopharmacology Bulletin, 33,* 345–354.

Bulimia Nervosa

☐ Introduction

This section focuses on the eating disorder bulimia nervosa. Although its sister condition, anorexia nervosa, has been the source of interest and study for at least 100 years, bulimia nervosa was described as a distinct diagnostic entity only in 1979 by Gerald Russell, working at the Maudsley Hospital in London. In his initial description, Russell characterized bulimia nervosa as an ominous variant of anorexia nervosa. Many of his cases were individuals of low weight or with prior low weight who would have also met criteria for anorexia nervosa although they binge ate and purged. In the current nomenclature, such individuals would be classified as having binge-purge anorexia nervosa rather than bulimia nervosa. Therefore, an important point to consider when reading these vignettes is that most patients with bulimia nervosa are of normal weight or overweight, while those with anorexia nervosa are clearly underweight. However, some bulimic women clearly are near the bottom of what we would consider an acceptable weight range, and some teeter on the brink of developing full blown anorexia nervosa. In reading these vignettes, consider the additional following points:

1) Most people know that individuals with anorexia nervosa feel fat even when they are very thin, and worry a great deal about their weight and shape. How important are these issues in the diagnosis of bulimia nervosa?

2) Bulimia nervosa is subdivided into two groups—those who engage

in purging compensatory behaviors for binge eating (e.g., vomiting or taking laxatives, diuretics, or water pills) and those who engage in non-purging compensatory behaviors (e.g., fasting, excessive exercise). Into which subgroup would this patient fall, and what are the compensatory behaviors in which she engages?

3) Many patients with bulimia nervosa have other associated problems which may predate the onset of their eating disorder or develop in the context of the eating disorder. This includes higher than expected rates of major depression, anxiety disorders, certain forms of personality disorders, and substance misuse or abuse disorders. Which of these are problematic for the individual portrayed in these vignettes?

☐ Diagnostic Criteria
(DSM-IV)

A. Recurrent episodes of binge eating. An episode of binge eating is characterized by both of the following:
   1) Eating, in a discrete period of time (e.g., within any two-hour period) an amount of food that is definitely larger than most people would eat during a similar period of time and under similar circumstances
   2) A sense of lack of control over eating during the episode (e.g., a feeling that one cannot stop eating or control what or how much one is eating)
B. Recurrent inappropriate compensatory behavior in order to prevent weight gain, such as self-induced vomiting; misuse of laxatives, diuretics, enemas, or other medications; fasting; or excessive exercise.
C. The binge eating and inappropriate compensatory behaviors both occur, on average, at least twice a week for three months.
D. Self-evaluation is unduly influenced by body shape and weight.
E. The disturbance does not occur exclusively during episodes of Anorexia Nervosa.

Specify type:

Purging Type: during the current episode of Bulimia Nervosa, the person has regularly engaged in self-induced vomiting or the misuse of laxatives, diuretics, or enemas.

Non-purging Type: during the current episode of Bulimia Nervosa, the person has used other inappropriate compensatory behaviors, such as fasting or excessive exercise, but has not regularly engaged in self-induced vomiting or the misuse of laxatives, diuretics, or enemas.

☐ The Stories

I

Judy Rawling sat with her friend, Jeannine Struthers, on her screened in porch. They were both having coffee, and a plate of cookies rested on the table between them. Jeannine had invited Judy over because Jeannine was upset about a problem with her daughter and didn't know where to turn. Jeannine had told Judy something of the problem earlier that week, but had decided to tell her the whole thing. Judy was a person she trusted a great deal, and Jeannine had found that her husband didn't understand the problem.

Jeannine began tentatively, "Judy, thanks so much for coming over. I really needed to talk to someone, and Barry just doesn't listen to me. He doesn't see it as an issue. Frankly, I don't think he understands it because he is a man. Anyway, as I told you Tuesday, I'm worried about Jennifer. Actually, I've been worried about her for months. She just isn't her same old self. As you know, she's still here even though she is going to community college. Also, as you know, she was doing fairly well in her studies, but things have really gone sour."

Judy genuinely wanted to help, and tried to understand. She reached across and placed her hand on her friend's arm. "Jeannine, I know this is hard for you to talk about, but tell me what's going on."

Jeannine continued, "Well, the first thing I worried about was the irritability. She'd snap at the slightest problem. She was always such an easygoing kid in high school but now if I say something wrong she jumps right on me. She seems to get mad at the slightest thing. She seems so sad all the time. She never jokes around like she used to. She was always the one in the family that made everybody laugh around the dinner table, which reminds me, she never eats with us anymore. We haven't had a meal with Jennifer since, well, I can't remember when, but months ago. But she's eating though. Lots. I'll find boxes of things missing. For example, this morning I went to open the breakfast cereal and couldn't find the box, which I had picked up at the grocery store yesterday. It wasn't there. I asked Barry if he knew where it was, and I thought that maybe I had misplaced it, but later I found it in the trash, completely empty. That sort of thing happens all the time now. I couldn't understand how she seemed to be eating all this food, not with us but on her own, and yet she seemed to be losing weight. Now I think I've figured it out."

Judy was concerned and intrigued, "Go on."

"I think she's vomiting the food. Earlier this week when I was cleaning the toilet I noticed bits of red colored food and other stuff around the rim of the toilet and on the floor. Someone had wiped it up but they hadn't gotten all of it. I cleaned it up not thinking much about it, but then the next day there was more there, although not nearly as much, just a little bit. I think she's throwing up the food she's eating. I think it's called bulimia nervosa, bulimia, or something."

Judy recalled seeing a T.V. show about bulimia. She knew it involved girls or women who would eat a lot of food and then throw it up to get rid of it so they wouldn't gain weight. She had heard about this but never knew much about it before the T.V. show. She said, "Jeannine, I saw a T.V. show about this a few weeks ago. It's something that girls do. They are worried about their weight so they eat and throw up, but they also diet a lot. The don't eat at other times."

Jeannine said, "Yes, I saw the same program." She continued, "It never occurred to me it might be Jennifer. She is using laxatives, which they talked about on the program. I started going through the trash this week and I found two boxes of laxatives that she bought at Custer's Drug Store. The empty boxes were in the sack with a receipt, shoved into the bottom of the trash. I think it's dangerous."

"Have you asked her about it?" asked Judy.

"That's why I asked you to come over today," said Jeannine looking more tense and concerned by the minute. "Barry wasn't home last night and I told her I had something I wanted to talk to her about. We sat down here on the porch. I told her I was worried about her, that I had found out she was vomiting, and the boxes of laxatives. I said that I was worried about her and that I wanted her to get some help."

"Well, what did she say?" asked Judy.

"She exploded at me. She told me it was none of my business and that she didn't vomit. She told me that I should leave her alone, that I didn't understand her, have never understood her, and that if I didn't leave her alone she was going to move out. Then she ran out of the house and didn't come back until the middle of the night. I was so worried about her. I stayed up all night sitting in a chair waiting for her to come in. When she came in and saw me, she yelled at me again and then went to her room. She left again early this morning. I haven't seen her since."

II

Jennifer was feeling desperate. Her mother had confronted her the night before about the vomiting and the laxatives. She thought she had been so careful to hide what she was doing, and hoped that no one would ever know her secret. (I should have known that eventually somebody would find out.) She was feeling tired, depressed, embarrassed, and very worried. She didn't know what she could do. (I know I shouldn't do it, but I just can't stop. If I do I'll get fat and I couldn't stand that. It would be better to die.) She had lied to her mother about the vomiting and laxatives. She had to. It was her only choice. (Having to lie about things is part of my life now. Where I've been, why I can't go out, where the food has gone.)

Her life was going downhill. She and Richard had been getting close in the fall. Now they had drifted apart. (He hasn't called in over a month.) When she had last talked with him he had been angry because she refused to go out one night for dinner. Stacy, her closest friend, also seemed further away lately, but what could she expect? If they did anything together it was after Stacy called, not because she called Stacy. Food had become the most important thing in her life. She thought about it all day long.

Jennifer had settled into a routine. She would get up in the morning, weigh herself, and try on the same pair of jeans. The combination of her weight, and the tightness of her jeans, which she took as a body shape measurement, would determine the tenor of the entire day. If she stayed the same, things would be tolerable. If she lost a bit of weight things would be okay. If her weight was higher, at all higher, the day was a disaster. Today she had weighed 123 pounds. She was 5'5" tall.

Regardless of her weight and the tightness of her jeans, she knew that her eating was difficult to control, so she put off eating anything at all as long as she could during the day. She never ate breakfast and rarely ate lunch. Then in the late afternoon or evening, after leaving school, she would either binge eat on the way home on fast food, or get home before her parents and binge eat and throw up there. This was going to be a fast food day.

She stopped first at McDonald's, ordered two chocolate milk shakes, a large order of fries, and two quarter pounders with cheese. (The people working at the restaurant will assume I am picking up food for two people.) She specifically asked for two napkins and two straws—which would have been given to her anyway—just to make sure they knew the food wasn't all for her. She then ate this food while driving for ten minutes, feeling numb and out of control, before pulling into Taco Bell. (It is hard sometimes to eat while you are driving.) It was particularly difficult when there were many cars, and she had almost had accidents on several occasions. She ordered several items at Taco Bell, again in a form to suggest that she was buying food for two people and again drove around, working her way toward home. She stopped at the Standard Station on the corner, parked by the women's bathroom and went in. When she came out five minutes later she had gotten rid of the food and, to make sure, had taken ten laxatives before returning to the car. She felt sad, down, and somewhat ashamed, but relieved that she had been able to get rid of the food before it was absorbed—before it could make her fat.

The previous week she had been very frightened. She had noticed blood in her vomit and wondered if this meant that she was going to die. It had cleared up after a couple of days, however, and she had felt better about it. She had noticed though that her hair had been thinning in recent months, that she had little energy, and, although she didn't understand why, some days her cheeks seemed puffy. She also noticed that when she got up at night to have diarrhea after taking the laxatives she usually felt dizzy and lightheaded and would hold on to the wall when going back to bed so she didn't collapse or faint. Until she had been confronted by her mother, the only person that had suspected the vomiting was her dentist. During a dental exam about two months before, he had told her that her teeth appeared eroded and asked if she might be having trouble with a hiatal hernia, or with vomiting for some other reason. She of course denied it and he had not mentioned it again.

☐ Discussion

This individual clearly has an eating disorder. The options, therefore, would be anorexia nervosa, bulimia nervosa, or eating disorders not otherwise specified (EDNOS), the latter of which includes binge eating disorder, characterized by the presence of binge eating without compensatory behaviors. The crucial variable for the diagnosis of anorexia nervosa that is lacking in this case is low weight. Additionally, she engages in compensatory purging behavior, and therefore does not meet criteria for binge eating disorder. Focusing in on the criteria for bulimia nervosa, her symptoms are clear. She engages in binge eating episodes characterized by a sense of loss of control, and eats large amounts of food in a discrete period of time. She clearly is preoccupied with weight and shape issues, engages in compensatory behaviors, and if we assume that she couples binge eating with the compensatory behaviors at least twice a week and has done so for at least three months, she then satisfies criteria for bulimia nervosa.

This individual also appears to have a number of other problems, with depression being most prominent. She may also satisfy criteria for major depressive disorder, although the data presented are incomplete for the assessment of that diagnosis.

The differential diagnosis here is relatively straightforward. Anorexia nervosa is excluded because of her weight, and binge eating disorder by the presence of compensatory behaviors.

Relative to the binge eating, one must always consider the possibility that there is some organic problem that may cause someone to overeat. This happens rarely in the case of lesions of the central nervous system, such as tumors in the hypothalamus or the temporal lobe of the brain. There is no evidence that such an abnormality is present in this patient, and such problems are rare. One also must consider whether or not the compensatory behaviors are involuntary (e.g., secondary to a medical condition such as vomiting because of a hiatal hernia, which makes it easy for food to pass from the stomach back into the esophagus, or some other obstruction in the bowel which makes it difficult for the food to pass). Again, there is no medical history suggesting such a condition, and the patient voluntarily vomits, suggesting that the etiology is not organic.

The clinical presentation of this case is actually fairly typical. Bulimia nervosa occurs primarily in women (approximately nine out of ten cases), with a mean age of onset in late adolescent or the early adult years (on average around age 17 or 18). Bulimia nervosa tends to be more common among individuals who live in western, industrialized societies such as the U.S. where there is an abundance of food and where a very high valence is placed on slimness as a model of attractiveness for women. Bulimia nervosa often first develops in the context of dieting. The usual pattern is that individuals with this disorder is symptomatic for several years before seeking treatment, and often comes for treatment not because of their eating symptoms per se but because they develop psychological, social, or medical complications.

As mentioned, it is fairly common for individuals who have bulimia nervosa to have premorbidly, or to develop during the course of the eating disorders, other psychiatric disorders including major depressive disorder, anxiety disorder, certain personality disorders (particularly Cluster B disorders such as borderline personality disorder), and substance abuse disorders (primarily involving alcohol). Because of such problems, psychosocial impairment is usually quite significant among these patients.

Individuals with bulimia nervosa experience marked family and social impairment. There are also a number of potentially serious medical complications. These include fluid imbalance and electrolyte abnormalities. Because of the purging behaviors, bulimic women may have dehydration, and develop deficiencies in electrolytes such as sodium, potassium, and chloride. Vomiting promotes the loss of dental enamel, which is irreversible. Bulimic individuals can develop fatal medical complications, including a ruptured stomach or esophagus, on rare occasions.

There is a fairly large treatment literature on bulimia nervosa that has evolved over the last 20 years. Treatment studies have developed along two main lines. First, there have been a variety of psychotherapeutic approaches. In the controlled treatment studies that are available the form of therapy that is best established is cognitive behavioral therapy.

The other parallel literature has focused on the use of antidepressant drugs. Antidepressant drugs were originally tried because of the observation that many patients with bulimia nervosa were also depressed. However, the literature suggests that individuals with bulimia nervosa may respond to antidepressants whether or not they have comorbid depression. The class of drugs that have been most extensively evaluated are the serotonin reuptake inhibitors, in particular fluoxetine hydrochloride, which is now FDA approved for the treatment of bulimia nervosa, at a dosage range of up to 60 mg a day. Of interest, high dose therapy, appears to work better than the lower dose therapy that is used in depression treatment.

Several recent studies suggest that there may be some advantage, when both are available, to combine cognitive behavioral therapy with medication.

Although the outcome for such treatments are good, there is a significant subgroup of patients who remain symptomatic after these treatments, and are at risk for relapse. Also, cognitive behavioral therapy for bulimia nervosa is not available in most treatment settings. Therefore, there is a disparity between what has been developed in controlled treatment trials and what is usually available in most communities.

☐ Points for Further Discussion

1) Many patients purge by self-inducing vomiting while others use large doses of laxatives. How do laxatives work as a purging mechanism?

2) It is very rare to see an individual with bulimia nervosa with an age of onset beyond age 40. Why would this be true?

3) Since we know that bulimia nervosa often develops in the context of dieting in an adolescent or young adult woman who is actually of normal weight but feels uncomfortable with her body weight, what could be done to prevent the development of bulimia nervosa?

References

American Psychiatric Association. (1994). *Diagnostic and statistical manual of mental disorders* (4th ed.). Washington, DC: Author.

Suggested Readings

Andersen, A. E., & Holman, J. E. (1997). Males with eating disorders: Challenges for treatment and research. *Psychopharmacology Bulletin, 33*, 391–397.

Batal, H., Johnson, M., Lehman, D., Steele, A., & Mehler, P. S. (1998). Bulimia: A primary care approach. *Journal of Womens Health, 7*, 211–220.

Casper, R. C. (1998). Recognizing eating disorders in women. *Psychopharmacology Bulletin, 34*, 267–269.

Crow, S. J., & Mitchell, J. E. (1996). Integrating cognitive therapy and medications in treating bulimia nervosa. *Psychiatric Clinics of North America, 19*, 755–760.

Howard, C. E., & Porzelius, L. K. (1999). The role of dieting in binge eating disorder: Etiology and treatment implications. *Clinical Psychology Review, 19*, 25–44.

Jarry, J. L. (1998). The meaning of body image for women with eating disorders. *Canadian Journal of Psychiatry, 43*, 367–374.

Kaye, W. H., Gendall, K., & Kye, C. (1998). The role of the central nervous system in the psychoneuroendocrine disturbances of anorexia and bulimia nervosa. *Psychiatric Clinics of North America, 21*, 381–396.

Mayer, L. E., & Walsh, B. T. (1998). The use of selective serotonin reuptake inhibitors in eating disorders. *Journal of Clinical Psychiatry, 59*, 28–34.

Mitchell, J. E., Crow, S., Peterson, C. B., Wonderlich, S., & Crosby, R. D. (1998). Feeding laboratory studies in patients with eating disorders: A review. *International Journal of Eating Disorders, 24*, 115–124.

Powers, P. S. (1999). Osteoporosis and eating disorders. *Journal of Pediatric and Adolescent Gynecology, 12*, 51–57.

Robin, A. L., Gilroy, M., & Dennis, A. B. (1998). Treatment of eating disorders in children and adolescents. *Clinical Psychology Review, 18*, 421–446.

Schmidt, U., & Treasure, J. (1997). Eating disorders and the dental practitioner. *European Journal of Prosthodontic Restoration Dentistry, 5*, 161–167.

Sokol, M. S., Steinberg, D., & Zerbe, K. J. (1998). Childhood eating disorders. *Current Opinion in Pediatrics, 10*, 369–377.

Steiner, H., & Lock, J. (1998). Anorexia nervosa and bulimia nervosa in children and adolescents: A review of the past 10 years. *Journal of the American Academy of Child and Adolescent Psychiatry, 37*, 352–359.

Sunday, S. R., & Halmi, K. A. (1997). Eating behavior and eating disorders: The interface between clinical research and clinical practice. *Psychopharmacology Bulletin, 33*, 373–379.

Vaz, F. J. (1998). Outcome of bulimia nervosa: Prognostic indicators. *Journal of Psychsomatic Research, 45*, 391–400.

Walsh, B. T., & Devlin, M. J. (1998). Eating disorders: Progress and problems. *Science, 280*, 1387–1390.

Walsh, B. T., & Kahn, C. B. (1997). Diagnostic criteria for eating disorders: Current concerns and future directions. *Psychopharmacology Bulletin, 33*, 369–372.

Wiseman, C. V., Harris, W. A., & Halmi, K. A. (1998). Eating disorders. *Medical Clinics of North America, 82*, 145–159.

Wolfe, B. E., Metzger, E., & Jimerson, D. C. (1997). Research update on serotonin function in bulimia nervosa and anorexia nervosa. *Psychopharmacology Bulletin, 33,* 345–354.

Ziolko, H. U. (1996). Bulimia: A historical outline. *International Journal of Eating Disorders, 20,* 345–358.

X IMPULSE-CONTROL DISORDERS NOT OTHERWISE CLASSIFIED

This grouping of disorders is rather heterogeneous and includes several different types of disorders that involve giving in to or acting on temptations or impulses. The results of these behaviors are either self-damaging (trichotillomania, pathological gambling), or are potentially harmful to others (pyromania, kleptomania, intermittent explosive disorder). Pyromania involves fire setting for psychological reasons, kleptomania is recurrent theft that is not engendered by the financial need to do so, and where the pleasure is in the act itself, and intermittent explosive disorder involves recurrent episodes of aggressive behavior that result in physical harm to others or property damage. We will illustrate trichotillomania and pathological gambling.

21

CHAPTER

Pathological Gambling

☐ Introduction

The primary feature of pathological gambling is a pattern of recurrent gambling behaviors (e.g., betting on cards, horse racing) that causes significant psychosocial impairment. People may develop severe financial problems, lose their job, and suffer significant problems in relationships with family and friends.

In reading the following stories, pay particular attention to the following issues:

1) What is the pattern of the development of the problem? How does it change over time?
2) The term "chasing" is sometimes used in describing pathological gambling. What do you think this term means, and why?

☐ Diagnostic Criteria
(DSM-IV)

A. Persistent and recurrent maladaptive gambling behavior as indicated by five (or more) of the following:
   1) Is preoccupied with gambling (e.g., preoccupied with reliving past gambling experiences, handicapping or planning the next venture, or thinking of ways to get money with which to gamble).
   2) Needs to gamble with increasing amounts of money in order to achieve the desired excitement.

3) Has repeated unsuccessful efforts to control, cut back, or stop gambling.
4) Is restless or irritable when attempting to cut down or stop gambling.
5) Gambles as a way of escaping from problems or of relieving a dysphoric mood (e.g., feelings of helplessness, guilt, anxiety, depression).
6) After losing money gambling, often returns another day to get even ("chasing" one's losses)
7) Lies to family members, therapist, or others to conceal the extent of involvement with gambling.
8) Has committed illegal acts such as forgery, fraud, theft, or embezzlement to finance gambling.
9) Has jeopardized or lost a significant relationship, job, or educational or career opportunity because of gambling.
10) Relies on others to provide money to relieve a desperate financial situation caused by gambling.
B. The gambling behavior is not better accounted for by a Manic Episode.

☐ The Stories

I

Jack Lansing was born in the late 60s. He was the third of three children with two older sisters. His father, Peter, an engineer, worked for a consulting firm. His mother, Janet, was a grade school teacher. He enjoyed a basically happy, healthy childhood. He was well liked by his friends, a decent athlete, and an above average student. He was also known as something of a risk taker. He liked excitement. He was always the first one to accept a dare. When he was 13 he fractured his right lower leg when someone bet him he couldn't climb up in a tree far enough to retrieve an errant Frisbee. He made it to the Frisbee, but the trip down proved hazardous, and he fell the last 15 feet. He loved the excitement of computer games and frequently played with friends and, although the amounts were small, he and his friends would frequently bet on the outcomes of these games. Sometimes a quarter, sometimes a dollar. He saw a movie when he was 14 in which men made their living playing poker and other card games. He was excited by this and checked out some books at the library about the subject. He taught himself how to play all the best card games and introduced his circle of friends to cards as well. His sophomore year in high school he started a weekly poker game. Jack was the organizer and the main sponsor of the activity. Sometimes $20 or $30 would change hands in the course of an evening. Jack found that he thought about these games often, replaying hands in his mind and anticipating the next session. The gambling never got out of hand, however.

He graduated from high school in the top third of his class, decided on an engineering career like his father, and began at the state university. He easily settled into life in the dormitory and into his classes, and things seemed to be going well. Within a month of starting school he had again organized a poker game with other guys from his dormitory. He also made his first trip to a Native American gaming casino on a reservation located about 30 miles from town. He liked blackjack, and developed a habit of making the bus trip to the casino at least once a weekend, sometimes twice, and then later occasionally during the week as well.

His parents were generous with tuition support and other funds, but he found these trips to the casino increasingly expensive. At first he imposed a firm limit on himself; he would not continue to gamble if he lost $20. It would generally take him a fairly short period of time to lose this amount, although he improved his skill significantly and took great pride in breaking even or making a profit. One Saturday afternoon he made $170. He would replay that session in his mind many times in the months ahead. He found he was thinking about gambling much of the time, either the poker game or the trips to the casino or other kinds of gambling which had crept into his life, such as betting on college basketball games.

When he first began asking his parents for extra money, they became concerned, so he decided he couldn't do that any longer and instead took a part time job at a local drug store. He had begun to date a girl named Janie, also a college freshman, who was interested in business. She was bright, perky, outgoing, and lots of fun to be with. They enjoyed movies or hiking in the woods on the weekends. During the first six months of college they became quite close and their relationship was such that they talked about the possibility of eventually marrying and having children.

However, Janie was becoming increasingly worried about Jack. He would frequently cancel dates on the weekends and sometimes during the week saying he had other things to do. She knew he gambled, and she increasingly suspected that this was the behavior that kept him away from her. She also knew he was working too many hours, was frequently too tired to attend class, and that his grades were suffering.

Jack was getting worried as well. He still got a sense of being high and excited when he gambled. And he found he could no longer stick to his limit; the limit had been increased from $20 to $30, and then to $50, but now he sometimes would stay long after he'd lost his limit, trying desperately to win his losses back. He sometimes would return to the casino the next day, again trying desperately to make up for his previous losses.

One Saturday he found he was totally out of funds but knowing that he would be receiving a paycheck the next Wednesday, he wrote what he knew was a bad check, thinking that he could cover it before it cleared the bank. This became an ongoing pattern, and he soon was spending money on a regular basis before he was paid. He also borrowed money from some of his friends including his roommate, but they tired of this behavior rather quickly and refused to loan him any more. Janie flatly refused to loan him anything, and after he asked her again a week later the relationship deteriorated further. She told him she thought he had a problem, that he needed to get help, and that she didn't want to watch him destroy himself.

At this point he decided to quit gambling altogether, and made a promise to himself that he would no longer go to the casino, organize the poker games, or bet on college basketball or anything else. He had made this promise to himself on Sunday after losing $300 over Saturday and Sunday at the casino, but on Wednesday he was organizing the poker game and on Thursday night was back at the casino, using more money that he had obtained using a bad check.

Final exams were a week away. He had been attending class only sporadically, had not finished any of the papers that were required for the semester, had done little reading, and it was becoming increasingly clear to him that he was not going to make his grades and would not be able to stay in school. When he thought about the possible end of his academic career he became very unhappy and felt guilty. He discovered the one way to help these feelings was to go back to the casino and gamble, and then temporarily his dysphoria would lift.

II

Janie Trudeau had liked Jack from the beginning. He was a good looking, good natured guy who was lots of fun to be around, had lots of friends, and had a quick, warm smile that made her feel great. He always had lots of energy, always wanted to do things, was always on the move. They had hit if off right away. They had many things in common—the love of the outdoors, a love for cinema—and their relationship had just clicked.

She had known from the beginning of their relationship that he liked to gamble. In the fall she would occasionally sit in on the poker sessions he had with his friends, although frequently she would get bored after an hour or so and go back to her own dormitory. She found these episodes fun and exciting, as did he, but only for a while. It became increasingly clear to her that he couldn't stop himself when it came to gambling, that he had to do it. Things went downhill from there. She knew he lied to her about where he was going and why he couldn't do things. He seemed more edgy and uncomfortable. He never studied with her anymore (I wonder if he studies at all.) He was moody and irritable. (It's probably the gambling.) Then he tried to borrow money from her. That was the last straw. She was hurt and humiliated. She told him that she was going to have to step back and think about herself, and that if he wanted to destroy himself that was okay, but she didn't want to be part of it.

She had met Jack's parents twice. Once when they were in town to visit Jack she had had dinner with the three of them, and another time Jack had taken her home for the weekend. She debated in her mind whether or not to call Jack's parents and tell them about her concerns. She felt that this would violate her relationship with Jack and for the time being, at least, she decided against it.

☐ Discussion

It is clear in this scenario that this individual has crossed over from social gambling to pathological gambling, and is suffering the consequences of that financially, interpersonally, and academically. He has attempted to exert control over his gambling behavior unsuccessfully, frequently loses control, and is "chasing" (e.g., trying to make up for his losses which have been escalating). He has also been writing bad checks and is working rather than attending classes so that he will have money to feed his habit.

When one encounters a person who is gambling in a pathological manner, one must always consider the possibility of the diagnosis of mania. There is no evidence of manic symptoms in this particular case. The gambling seems to be the isolated problem. Also, pathological gambling sometimes develops in those with depression as a means of soothing their depressed mood. This pattern is particularly common among women. However, although at the end of the story Jack seems to be using his gambling as a way to sooth his dysphoria, earlier in the course of the problem gambling seemed to be fueled more by the "high" he gets from the behavior.

Pathological gambling is a problematic behavioral disorder that develops usually in men, often with gambling antecedents during adolescence, that escalates and becomes out of the individual's control in adulthood. Such individuals find that they increase the frequency of their gambling and the amount that they lose while gambling, and begin to experience financial consequences of the gambling as well as other consequences such as occupational or academic failure, and impairment in interpersonal relationships, as well as guilt and low self-esteem.

Recent research suggests that pathological gambling is becoming far more common in the U.S. now that means of public gambling are much more widely available then they were one to two decades ago.

☐ Questions for Further Discussion

1) Think about your own behavior. Have you gambled before? Many of us have but usually infrequently and in a controlled way. Why does it get out of control for some individuals?
2) Do you think institutionalized gambling should be outlawed? What would be the pros and cons of such a law?
3) Should Janie call Jack's parents?
4) Why is the prevalence of pathological gambling changing in the United States?

☐ References

American Psychiatric Association. (1994). *Diagnostic and statistical manual of mental disorders* (4th ed.). Washington, DC: Author.

☐ Suggested Readings

Blaszczynski, A., & Silove, D. (1996). Pathological gambling: Forensic issues. *Australian and New Zealand Journal of Psychiatry, 30,* 358–369.

Crockford, D. N., & el-Guebaly, N. (1998). Psychiatric comorbidity in pathological gambling: A critical review. *Canadian Journal of Psychiatry, 43,* 43–50.

Cusack, J. R., Malaney, K. R., & DePry, D. L. (1993). Insights about pathological gamblers. "Chasing losses" in spite of the consequences. *Postgraduate Medicine, 93,* 169–179.

DeCaria, C. M., Hollander, E., Grossman, R., Wong C. M., Mosovich, S. A., & Cherkasky, S. (1996). Diagnostic neurobiology and treatment of pathological gambling. *Journal of Clinical Psychiatry, 57,* 80–84.

Griffiths, M. (1996). Pathological gambling: A review of the literature. *Journal of Psychiatric Mental Health Nursing 3*, 347–353.

Lopez Viets, V. C., & Miller, W. R. (1997). Treatment approaches for pathological gamblers. *Clinical Psychology Review, 17*, 689–702.

Miller, M. M. (1996). Medical approaches to gambling issues—I: The medical condition. *Wisconsin Medical Journal, 95*, 623–634.

Miller, M. M. (1996). Medical approaches to gambling issues—II: The medical response. *Wisconsin Medical Journal, 95*, 635–642.

Murray, J. B. (1993). Review of research on pathological gambling. *Psychology Reports, 72*, 791–810.

Rosenthan, R. J., & Lorenz, V. C. (1992). The pathological gambler as criminal offender. Comments on evaluation and treatment. *Psychiatric Clinics of North America, 15*, 647–660.

Spunt, B., Dupont, I., Lesieur, H., Liberty, H. J., & Hunt, D. (1998). Pathological gambling and substance misuse: A review of the literature. *Substance Use and Misuse, 33*, 2535–2560.

22

CHAPTER

Trichotillomania

☐ Introduction

The central feature of trichotillomania is pulling out one's hair. Hair from any body area can be pulled, although the top of the head is the most common sight. Stress seems to precipitate these pulling episodes, and a sense of reduced tension often results from them. Trichotillomania was first described over 100 years ago (and illusions to it date back to antiquity), but has only been receiving scrutiny by psychiatrists the last few decades. In reading the following scenarios, please consider the following:

1) What is Sharon doing during the times she pulls out her hair?
2) What are the ways that someone with trichotillomania can camouflage their hair loss?
3) Can you think of anything that Sharon can do that would help her gain control of the behavior?

☐ Diagnostic Criteria
(DSM-IV)

A. Recurrent pulling out of one's hair resulting in noticeable hair loss.
B. An increasing sense of tension immediately before pulling out the hair or when attempting to resist the behavior.

C. Pleasure, gratification, or relief when pulling out the hair.
D. The disturbance is not better accounted for by another mental disorder and is not due to a general medical condition (e.g., a dermatological condition).
E. The disturbance causes clinically significant distress or impairment in social, occupational, or other important areas of functioning.

☐ The Stories

I

Sharon Soland was a 36-year-old divorced female bank teller who lived in a high rise building about a mile from the bank in which she worked. Despite her single status she was basically happy. She loved her apartment which she had decorated in her favorite colors (deep blue and gray), loved to cook (sometimes traditional dishes such as northern Italian fare, or more adventurous creations—she particularly liked Moroccan cooking). She had several close female friends. She had some male friends as well, but didn't date. She actively avoided getting involved in any kind of romantic relationship, afraid someone would discover her secret.

It was a Thursday. She had worked late and had stopped to do some grocery shopping on the way home. She had also stopped in for some pastries at the corner delicatessen, and was now seated in front of the television eating dinner—a low calorie entrée that she had just microwaved. As she ate and watched a situation comedy on television, her left hand drifted up to her scalp, and only half aware of what she was doing, she searched out what seemed to be particularly thick or stiff hairs, and one at a time pulled them out. As she did this she would absentmindedly inspect each hair, paying particular attention to the hair follicle, and would take the hair and run it back and forth over her lips, glancing again at the television as she did so, and occasionally taking a bite of food. (Why am I doing this? I'm going to be bald as a basketball. I've got to stop this.) She promptly took her left hand and stuck it in the crevice of the left-hand side of her chair, immobilizing it. She returned to watching the television show and finishing her dinner. As she became engrossed in the program and in eating, her left hand drifted up to the top of her head and once again began searching her hair.

This pattern seemed to reoccur frequently, and she again decided she needed to do something about it. She was particularly likely to pull her hair when feeling stressed about something (like when my boss says something to me.) She discovered long ago that the pulling had a soothing effect on her. She didn't feel any pain. At times her scalp seemed to itch and this seemed to be relieved by the hair pulling. She had been doing this for years, and although she had adopted a hairstyle that allowed her to cover the bald spot by combing her hair to the side, she nonetheless had lost a great deal of hair.

Frustrated with herself she got up from the chair, went into the bathroom, took her comb and combed the hair to the side that had been covering the bald spot. Leaning forward she could see the bald spot now. It was about 3 × 4 inches, circular, and a little asymmetrical toward the left. Sometimes the bald patch got larger and sometimes smaller. She was never able to control her behavior sufficiently for it to go away completely.

She had begun to notice some odd things now. The hair around the edge of the bald spot where she usually pulled had changed texture and color. It seemed darker and coarser than her other hair, which concerned her.

She thought back over the years of dealing with this problem and some of the things she tried to control. There was a period when she would force herself to wear rubber gloves when she was in the house. She found that she had more difficulty pulling and was less likely to pull when she wore them, but she couldn't keep wearing them all the time. For a while she actually tied a bell to her wrist but that didn't work either. She also tried coating her hair with petroleum jelly thinking that if she made her hair slick it would be more difficult to pull, but this was messy and really didn't work very well anyway.

She returned to the living room through her bedroom, passed a dresser drawer stuffed with silk scarves, which she used to cover her head at times, a closet loaded with hats of all descriptions and colors, and four model heads, each of which held a wig. Sometimes she just couldn't get her hair to lay right and would wear a wig instead.

(Thank God for Joyce.) Joyce was Joyce Crammer at the "Cut & Curl" shop downtown. Joyce owned this little shop, and specialized in people who had trichotillomania. Sharon had heard about her from a support group. She was the person who helped you find a hairstyle that would cover your bald spot. She was expensive but well worth it and had given Sharon a style that allowed her, for the most part to feel fairly assured about how she looked, although she still had to be very careful to avoid going out on windy days and usually ended up wearing a scarf if she was going to be outside. No one but Joyce knew her secret, and she wished to keep it that way.

Sitting in the living room in front of the T.V. she thought over this problem. (Why do I do it? It makes me so mad at myself? Why don't I have any self-control?) This is a pattern she repeated almost every evening—condemning herself for doing this thing that she didn't seem to be able to control.

II

Joyce greeted Sharon with a friendly wave. Joyce owned the "Cut & Curl," and had for 25 years. Joyce was a sturdy African-American woman of about 50 who had a bubbly personality and loved to talk with people. Sharon was somewhat reserved but always liked seeing Joyce because Joyce could get anyone to talk. This was helpful, because it was very hard for Sharon to let anyone see her head.

"How have you been the last two weeks?" inquired Joyce as she assessed the current level of damage to the top of Sharon's head.

"Really good actually. Things are going well at the bank. I got a raise. I went out with Kim shopping over the weekend."

Joyce was one of those people who could work and talk at the same time. "Buy anything?"

"Well, I did pick up a cute jacket but I also bought two scarves." Sharon and Joyce both laughed. Buying scarves was a standard joke between them.

Joyce worked away with her scissors and comb. "You know, one of my customers told me yesterday about a new drug treatment they are using for this hair pulling thing. She got it from a doctor at the university who sees people who pull their hair. It's evidently a drug for depression but it also may help people with hair pulling. Have you ever heard of that?"

Sharon responded, "No, not at all, but it's hard to believe that a drug could make you not want to pull your hair unless it made you fall asleep."

☐ Discussion

This individual appears to satisfy criteria for trichotillomania. She clearly has noticeable hair loss (which she attempts to camouflage), reports decreasing tension and a sense of gratification when pulling, and tension before pulling. Clearly she has attempted to resist the behavior. We have no evidence of any other Axis I or Axis II disorder or of any primary skin problem. She clearly is distressed by the condition, and her fear of discovery keeps her from involving herself in any kind of romantic relationship.

People with trichotillomania often pull in situations when they are not completely aware of what they are doing, such as when they are reading, watching television, or distracted in some way. Although the preceding tension and sense of relief after pulling are part of the diagnostic criteria, research has shown that some patients do not have tension and subsequent tension reduction, but simply pull. Examining the hair root and pulling the strand between the lips or teeth is fairly commonly reported as is eating hair which can result in the development of a gastric trichobezoar (hairball) in some cases. Sometimes people with trichotillomania will pull hair off dolls or threads from sweaters. The disorder can begin in childhood, adolescence, or adulthood. Although good prevalence figures are not available, estimates suggest that 1–2% of individuals develop trichotillomania and that the disorder is more common in women then men. The differential diagnosis one must consider is primary dermatological conditions such as alopecia areata or male pattern baldness, or hair pulling as part of a psychotic disorder such as schizophrenia.

Some recent research has suggested certain effective treatments for this condition. Serotonin reuptake inhibitors appear to be effective for some but not all patients. There is also some evidence that endogenous opiate antagonists such as Naltrexone may suppress trichotillomania in some individuals (perhaps by taking away the pleasure associated with the behavior). Various behavioral and cognitive behavioral strategies for treating these patients have also been developed, but have not been adequately tested empirically.

☐ Questions for Further Discussion

1) This disorder is classified as an impulsive control disorder. Do you think this behavior is really impulsive, or perhaps compulsive?
2) Some people with trichotillomania ingest their hair and develop a hairball in their stomach. Do you think there would be any possible medical complications of this?

☐ References

American Psychiatric Association. (1994). *Diagnostic and statistical manual of mental disorders* (4th ed). Washington, DC: Author.

☐ Suggested Readings

Bouwer, C., & Stein, D. J. (1998). Trichobezoars in trichotillomania: Case report and literature overview. *Psychsomatic Medicine, 60,* 658–660.

Christenson, G. A., & Crow, S. J. (1996). The characterization and treatment of trichotillomania. *Journal of Clinical Psychiatry, 57,* 42–49.

Jaspers, J. P. (1996). The diagnosis and psychopharmacological treatment of trichotillomania: A review. *Pharmacopsychiatry, 29,* 115–120.

Keuthen, N. J., O'Sullivan, R. L., & Sprich-Buckminster, S. (1998). Trichotillomania: Current issues in conceptualization and treatment. *Psychotherapy and Psychosomatics, 67,* 202–213.

Long, E. S., & Miltenberger, R. G. (1998). A review of behavioral and pharmacological treatments for habit disorders in individuals with mental retardation. *Journal of Behavioral Therapy and Experimental Psychiatry, 29,* 143–156.

Mansueto, C. S., Stemberger, R. M., Thomas, A. M., & Golomb, R. G. (1997). Trichotillomania: A comprehensive behavioral model. *Clinical Psychology Review, 17,* 567–577.

Minichiello, W. E., O'Sullivan, R. L., Osgood-Hynes, D., & Baer, L. (1994). Trichotillomania: Clinical aspects and treatment strategies. *Harvard Review of Psychiatry, 1,* 336–344.

Stein, D. J., Simeon, D., Cohen, L. J., & Hollander, E. (1995). Trichotillomania and obsessive-compulsive disorder. *Journal of Clinical Psychiatry, 56,* 28–35.

Sullivan, J. R., & Kossard, S. (1998). Acquired scalp alopecia. Part 1: A review. *Australas Journal of Dermatology, 39,* 207–221.

Yanchick, J. K., Barton, T. L., & Kelly, M. W. (1994). Efficacy of fluoxetine in trichotillomania. *Annuals of Pharmacotherapy, 28,* 1245–1246.

XI PERSONALITY DISORDERS

In DSM-IV, personality disorders are placed on a separate Axis from the other disorders we have discussed thus far: Axis II. This special classification reflects the fact that personality disorders are viewed differently and in general are more controversial than many of the Axis I forms of psychopathology. In particular, there is much sentiment that the categorical approach to diagnosis that has been so effective in improving our understanding of Axis I conditions may be misleading when it comes to personality disorders, given the fact that much research suggests that the personality disorders as used in the DSM system are not really distinct entities. Indeed, they tend to cluster into three groupings. If a person meets diagnostic criteria for one disorder they not uncommonly also meet criteria for two, three, or four others, suggesting a lack of discrete boundaries among them, and raising questions regarding the validity of the constructs. Also, much research suggests that many of the traits that we see in patients with personality disorders exist on a continuum with normal personality traits. Viewing personality traits as continuous variables may be more useful than a categorical approach (normal or abnormal). Nonetheless, personality problems clearly represent important clinical issues.

We will illustrate two of them. The first is borderline personality, a somewhat unfortunate term which was coined decades ago for reasons that are no longer relevant but which has stayed in the nomenclature because of its usage. The second is antisocial personality, or what is sometimes know as psychopathy or psychopathic personality.

Borderline Personality Disorder

☐ Introduction

Borderline personality disorder is a syndrome that has received considerable attention in the last 20–30 years and appears to account for a significant portion of visits to outpatient psychiatric facilities and days in psychiatric inpatient facilities. Individuals with borderline personality disorder are usually markedly impaired by their disorder, which is characterized by impulsivity and instability. The instability usually extends to their sense of self, their affective states (going from highs to lows very rapidly), and their interpersonal relationships (which can be characterized by intense closeness followed by distancing, and rejection). These individuals are very sensitive to any sense of criticism or threatened loss of interpersonal contact.

In the stories that follow, consider the following issues:

1) Pay attention to the issue of affective or mood instability. What changes do you see, if any, relative to affect over time? What seems to trigger these changes?
2) Notice how Penny's attitude toward Craig changes, and how quickly it changes.
3) What does Penny's sense of self seem to be? Does she seem to have a clear sense of who she is or how she affects people?

☐ Diagnostic Criteria
(DSM-IV)

A. A pervasive pattern of instability of interpersonal relationships, self-image and affects, and marked impulsivity beginning by early adulthood are present in a variety of contexts, as indicated by five (or more) of the following:

1) Frantic efforts to avoid real or imagined abandonment. **Note:** Do not include suicidal or self-mutilating behavior covered in Criterion 5.

2) A pattern of unstable and intense interpersonal relationships characterized by alternating between extremes of idealization and devaluation.

3) Identity disturbance: markedly and persistently unstable self-image or sense of self.

4) Impulsivity in at least two areas that are potentially self-damaging (e.g., spending, sex, substance abuse, reckless driving, binge eating). **Note:** Do not include suicidal or self-mutilating behavior covered in Criterion 5.

5) Recurrent suicidal behavior, gestures, or threats, or self-mutilating behavior.

6) Affective instability due to a marked reactivity of mood (e.g., intense episodic dysphoria, irritability, or anxiety usually lasting a few hours and only rarely more than a few days).

7) Chronic feelings of emptiness.

8) Inappropriate, intense anger or difficulty controlling anger (e.g., frequent displays of temper, constant anger, recurrent physical fights).

9) Transient, stress-related paranoid ideation or severe dissociative symptoms.

☐ The Stories

I

It had been a long evening studying in the library. Torts just didn't do it for Craig. He planned to head back to his apartment and call his family, but decided to stop by the "Men at Arms," the campus bar just off University Avenue, for a beer. He had never been able to figure out why this bar was so popular. It was always dark—you sometimes couldn't even see who was there—and the music was so loud that it hurt your ears. But it was a place everybody knew and a place where you could usually find your friends. Craig descended the stairs to the main area and immediately spotted Josh Lawrence, a friend and fellow law student, also second year, standing at the bar chatting with several of their friends. Craig crossed the dance area, dodging couples as he went, and put his hand on Josh's shoulder. Josh turned and greeted him.

"Craig ol' boy. Hitting the books late again?" asked Josh.

"Well, we do have the slight matter of the exam coming up on Friday. Quite frankly I don't think I'm ready yet."

"Craig, you never think you're ready but you always do great. Don't worry about it. Let's have a beer."

As his eyes became accustomed to the dark bar, Craig scanned the faces around the dance floor; some familiar, some not. He caught the eye of an attractive dark haired woman sitting directly across the dance floor from him. She was chatting in an animated fashion with two girlfriends, but clearly was watching him as well.

"Hey, Josh. Do you know who that dark haired girl across the floor is? The one in the red and blue sweater?"

Josh turned and gazed across the room. With a look of recognition on his face he turned to Craig, "Penny Marsh, grad student, anthropology. I actually went out with her once, but only once. She's trouble, man. She comes on real strong but it turns ugly real fast. I thought we were having a great evening, but then she just blew up for no apparent reason. Tom Richards used to date her. He told me about her one time. It turns out that she got mad at him one time and took a bunch of pills and had to go to the emergency room and have her stomach pumped. She's weird, man. I'd stay away from her. That was a while ago, though. Maybe she's okay now."

Craig drank his beer and chatted with his friends, occasionally glancing over his shoulder to where Penny sat with her entourage. She also kept him in view and after playing this visual game for a while he circled the dance floor, bent down, introduced himself, and asked her if she would like to dance. "Jumping Jack Flash" by the Rolling Stones was blaring from the jukebox. She smiled, said yes, and walked with him to the dance floor. (Oh, she's a great dancer and I like the way she dresses.)

Later that evening they were at Penny's apartment. Craig found Penny fun to be with. She was bright, affectionate (touching his arm, taking his hand), and seemed like a genuinely nice person. She had heard about him. She knew his reputation as one of the best law students. She had also heard about his career in college basketball as an undergraduate. She seemed to be almost in awe of him, and he found it very flattering.

They listened to music and chatted about mutual friends. She felt close and comfortable with him, it seemed to him. After an hour or so she became more romantic, kissing him and stroking his chest. They ended up having sex on the couch. Lying there next to her in the dimly lit room, Craig was surprised to notice that she had numerous scars on both of her arms. Most were at the wrist but some were further up her arm. Most were symmetrical across her arm but some were at odd angles. He also noticed scars on her abdomen and on the underside of her breasts. This worried him, and he remembered Josh's story of the overdose.

As they lay there together he decided to ask her about the scars and what they meant. As soon as the words were out of his mouth, she flew off the couch in a rage. She ran into the other room, quickly pulling on her clothes. She began to yell at him, "You asshole. What right do you have to ask me about anything? You couldn't understand me if you tried. You have no idea what I've been through. You're just like every other asshole around here."

Craig apologized, trying to find the right words to get her to calm down. When she picked up some CDs in their cases and hurled them against the wall, he decided it was time to leave. He got up and quickly dressed while she sulked on the couch.

"I'm sorry you're so upset. I'm sorry I said anything. Perhaps we can meet tomorrow for coffee and talk," he said and headed toward the door.

"Where are you going? Why are you leaving?" she asked in a pleading voice.

"You seem upset. I thought it would be better if you got some sleep."

"Oh great, use me for sex then leave. Dump me. Throw me away."

Craig was confused. It seemed now she didn't want him to leave. She started to cry and plead. "Please stay. I don't want to be alone."

II

After Craig left, Penny kicked off her shoes, grabbed a six pack of beer out of the refrigerator, turned on an old black and white movie on T.V., and sat down in the chair by the window. She was furious. She had been used again by another man. He had misled her, had lied to her, had led her on, and then dumped her. By the time she drank the fourth beer she was feeling somewhat more relaxed and less angry. (Why is life this way? Why do people treat me this way? I wonder sometimes if it's a plot. If people get together and talk about me and plan to treat me this way.) As she sat in the chair staring blankly at the screen, she felt a profound sense of emptiness and loneliness. It didn't make sense to her. (Why did people have to be such assholes in relationships? Why can't you ever trust people? Why did everyone use you and throw you away?) She thought back over her relationships for the last few years. She would meet someone, someone she at first thought was wonderful. She would fall for them, have sex with them, then they turn out to be an asshole just like everybody else.

☐ Discussion

As can be seen in the stories, borderline personality disorder is an extremely difficult problem to endure for the person with the disorder and for those in their environment. These stories illustrate several of the diagnostic criteria. This individual seems to engage in impulsive behavior (sex, possibly alcohol abuse), she has a sense of emptiness, she has rapid switches in mood. There seems to be a history of unstable, intense relationships. She seems to have a great fear of abandonment when Craig wishes to leave.

The impairment suffered by individuals with this disorder must be emphasized. They have a high rate of engaging in potentially self-injurious behaviors. Their thinking at times can be near psychotic.

This disorder seems to be quite prevalent among patients with personality disorders and may account for a significant minority of patients being seen in outpatient psychiatric clinics. The prevalence in the general population is probably around 2%. Such individuals are at high risk for other associated psychopathology, particularly substance related disorders and mood disorders. In the differential diagnosis, other personality disorders must be considered. Not uncommonly these individuals also will meet criteria for antisocial personality. The course of the disorder is highly variable. Usually evidence of the many core symptoms is present in adolescence, and symptoms are fairly severe during young adulthood. Some of these individuals seem to mellow, and to make a better adjustment as they age. However, the risk of death is high (in some series as high as 10%) from suicide or other dangerous behaviors such as driving while intoxicated.

Treatments for borderline personality disorder are only now being empirically tested. A form of psychotherapy called dialectical behavioral therapy (DBT) has been developed over the last decade that seems to be quite helpful for some of these patients. They also seem to benefit from supportive psychotherapy relationships, although such relationships are often difficult to maintain. At times, various medications are useful, particularly in the treatment of concurrent mood symptoms. In general, these are very difficult and frustrating patients to work with for psychiatrists and other mental health professionals.

☐ Questions for Further Discussion

1) Would you predict that Penny is having problems in graduate school? If so, what types of problems?
2) Why do you think that this condition often improves with age?
3) What medical problems might Penny develop because of her behavioral problems?

☐ References

American Psychiatric Association. (1994). *Diagnostic and statistical manual of mental disorders* (4th ed). Washington, DC: Author.

☐ Suggested Readings

Allen, D. M., & Farmer, R. G. (1996). Family relationships of adults with borderline personality disorder. *Comprehensive Psychiatry, 37,* 43–51.

Beatson, J. A. (1995). Long-term psychotherapy in borderline and narcissistic disorders: When it is necessary. *Australian and New Zealand Journal of Psychiatry, 29,* 591–597.

Coccaro, E. F. (1998). Clinical outcome of psychopharmacologic treatment of borderline and schizotypal personality disordered subjects. *Journal of Clinical Psychiatry, 59,* 30–37.

Goldstein, W. N. (1995). The borderline patient: Update on the diagnosis, theory, and treatment from a psychodynamic perspective. *American Journal of Psychotherapy, 49,* 317–337.

Gunderson, J. G., & Chu, J. A. (1993). Treatment implications of past trauma in borderline personality disorder. *Harvard Review of Psychiatry, 1,* 75–81.

Hirschfeld, R. M. (1997). Pharmacotherapy of borderline personality disorder. *Journal of Clinical Psychiatry, 58,* 48–52.

Hubbard, J. R., Saathoff, G. B., Bernardo, M. J., & Barnett, B. L. Jr. (1995). Recognizing borderline personality disorder in the family practice setting. *American Family Physician, 52,* 908–914.

Kjellander, C., Bongar, B., & King, A. (1998). Suicidality in borderline personality disorder. *Crisis, 19,* 125–135.

Miller, D. (1995). Diagnostic assessment and therapeutic approaches to borderline disorders in adolescents. *Adolescent Psychiatry, 20,* 237–252.

Nehls, N. (1998). Borderline personality disorder: Gender sterotypes, stigma, and limited system of care. *Issues in Mental Health Nursing, 19,* 97–112.

Paris, J. (1994). The etiology of borderline personality disorder: A biopsychosocial approach. *Psychiatry, 57,* 316–325.

Sansone, R. A., & Sansone, L. A. (1995). Borderline personality disorder. Interpersonal and behavioral problems that sabotage treatment success. *Postgraduate Medicine, 97,* 169–179.

Springer, T., & Silk, K. R. (1996). A review of inpatient group therapy for borderline personality disorder. *Harvard Review of Psychiatry, 3,* 268–278.

van der Kolk, B. A., Hostetler, A., Herron, N., & Fisler, R. E. (1994). Trauman and the development of borderline personality disorder. *Psychiatric Clinics of North America, 17,* 715–730.

Waldinger, R. J. (1993). The role of psychodynamic concepts in the diagnosis of borderline personality disorder. *Harvard Review of Psychiatry, 1,* 158–167.

24
CHAPTER

Antisocial Personality

☐ Introduction

The central pattern of those with antisocial personality disorder is an ongoing pervasive unwillingness to respect the rights of others and a repeated pattern of violating those rights. Many of these individuals therefore come into conflict with the law. Previous terms for this or related disorders include psychocopathy and sociopathy.

While reading the following scenarios consider the following points:

1) The gas station owner, Dick Jackson, likes Ben Steele for most of the story. He seems to admire him and is jealous of his travels. What do you think of Ben Steele?
2) What function does lying serve for Ben Steele? Why does he lie about the things he does?

☐ Diagnostic Criteria
(DSM-IV)

A. There is a pervasive pattern of disregard for a violation of the rights of others occurring since age 15 years, as indicated by three (or more) of the following:
   1) Failure to conform to social norms with respect to lawful behaviors as indicated by repeatedly performing acts that are grounds for arrest.

2) Deceitfulness, as indicated by repeated lying, use of aliases, or conning others for personal profit or pleasure.

3) Impulsivity or failure to plan ahead.

4) Irritability and aggressiveness, as indicated by repeated physical fights or assaults.

5) Reckless disregard for safety of self or others.

6) Consistent irresponsibility, as indicated by repeated failure to sustain consistent work behavior or honor financial obligations.

7) Lack of remorse as indicated by being indifferent to or rationalizing having hurt, mistreated, or stolen from another

B. The individual is at least age 18 years.

C. There is evidence of Conduct Disorder with onset before age 16 years.

D. The occurrence of antisocial behavior is not exclusively during the course of Schizophrenia or Manic Episode.

☐ The Stories

I

The two men sat in Sergeant Peterson's office. Dick Jackson slouched forward in a wooden chair and stared down into the styrofoam coffee cup he held, gradually turning it between his two hands. He felt much older than his 42 years, but not wiser. Sergeant Peterson sat across the desk trying to look alert and interested, occasionally glancing at the clock over Dick's right shoulder—still 40 minutes till lunch.

"Dick, it would really help if you start at the beginning and tell me the whole story. We're more likely to catch this guy if we really understand what happened. How did you meet this fella?" It was hard to get Dick Jackson to organize his story, but it was starting to come together.

Dick Jackson's mind went back to the afternoon about a month ago—was it a Thursday?—when he had first met Ben Steele. He was standing in front of his store having just filled the tank on a Buick station wagon—nice family from Ohio as he remembered—he'd given them directions about how to get back on the main road to Reno. It had been hot and boring, and he appreciated the interaction, even though it was brief. The days were hot—what else was new?—and always dusty. He then heard the throaty purr of a motorcycle coming in from the west, and he turned and watched the dark smear on the highway get larger as it kicked up dust. The whole thing was black; black motorcycle—low slung—and as it got closer, black jeans and shirt and long black hair and dark sunglasses came into view. As the cycle throttled down and pulled in front of the store, Dick saw a wide warm grin spread across the man's face, and he grinned back.

"Howdy! Got anything cold to drink in there?" asked the man on the bike.

Dick had taken to this man from the time he had seen him coming down the road. He wasn't sure why. The man seemed nice, had a nice smile, and a great motorcycle. Dick had always had an admiration for men who could strike out on their own and cut their own path. Even though he was on his own, he felt tied down to the store and station, to the memory of his wife, dead now five years, and to his mother in the nursing home ten miles away whom he tried to visit every Sunday. But in his mind, this man was different. This man didn't spend his evenings waiting for the sound of wheels on the gravel and sometimes a car honk to call him to the pumps. He had gone to Los Angeles once for a vacation with the wife. It cost lots of money, he didn't see any movie or TV stars, and he was glad to get home. This guy, he imagined, however, had been everywhere on that bike, everywhere Dick had never been.

The stranger confidently thrust out his hand and introduced himself: "Ben Steele. How are you doing?" The grin never left his face.

Dick introduced himself and told him what was available in the store to drink—Coke, Diet Coke, Mountain Dew, Coors beer, some other beer brands, and canned lemonade, all cold. Ben Steele swung his black booted foot over the bike and stood straight stretching his back and neck. Then in a slow measured tone said to Dick, "A beer— and let me buy you one." Dick nodded and the two men strode into the front of the store. There was a counter and cash register to the right, shelves stacked with cans and boxes to the back, and to the left a small seating area with two metal tables and four metal chairs around each, each with a glass star ashtray. The room was dull but clean— Dick swept it two or three times a day because of the dust, and the boredom.

Dick nodded toward the tables, "Have a seat. I'll get the beer."

Dick liked this guy, couldn't say exactly what he liked about him, but he did. He thought to himself, "He's friendly." Dick fished two bottles of beer out of the back cooler and brought them over to the table. He sat one down, twisted the cap off one, handed it to Ben, and picked up the other one for himself.

Ben took a long pull on the beer, sat it down sharply on the table, and grinned again. "Perfect. Just perfect. So, Dick, you own this place?"

Dick explained that he did, that he lived in the house connected to the back of the store. Ben nodded, "Are you here all alone?"

Dick said he was and explained that his wife had died. No, they hadn't had any children. Cancer. Breast cancer. Five years ago and he had lived alone here since then. He thought about moving on but never had and just sort of stayed.

Ben nodded, the smile draining from his face, "I'm a widower too, Dick. I lost my wife and two little girls in a plane crash about three years ago."

Dick said, "God. I'm sorry. How old were the girls?"

Ben said without hesitation, "Two and three. Just little and my wife young, too. Bad plane crash. Everyone was killed. I've never been the same."

Dick said, "Gosh," and didn't really know what else to say. He remembered how lost he had felt when his wife had died, but she'd taken a long time to die and he was with her every step of the way. Near the end she accepted it and so did he. It wasn't sudden like a plane crash, and not two little girls. "Gosh," said Dick again, shaking his head, wanting to say something helpful.

Ben added, "It changed everything."

Dick was trying to make conversation, trying to keep the man talking. "Well, how were things before?"

Ben sort of crinkled up one eye and his mind seemed to drift back to earlier times. "I was a stockbroker. Yep, a stockbroker in Chicago. I worked downtown in one of those big buildings. I was very happy. My wife and kids lived in the suburbs and I drove in everyday into the city and drove out every night. I worked hard. Some evenings I didn't get home until real late."

Dick tried to put everything together, "What are you doing here and why are you riding a motorcycle?"

Ben narrowed his vision and stared intently across the table at Dick. He thought for a moment, took another draw on the beer, and looked again. "I couldn't take it anymore after she and the kids were killed. I sold the house. I sold the cars. I sold the boat. I bought this bike. I hit the road to clear my head and I've been riding ever since. It really screwed me up. I suppose some day I'll go back to being a stockbroker again in Chicago, but for now I can't do it. Life just doesn't make sense to me. I just keep moving on hoping I'll find the answer."

Dick's mind tried to take all of this in. Traveling around the country for three years on a motorcycle. Think of the places this guy must have been? He could have been everywhere—L.A., New York, Canada, Mexico. He must have been everywhere to keep riding for three years. "Do you ever stop and work?"

Ben nodded as he took another draw on the beer and finished it, "Yep. I pick up jobs here and there just to give me something to do, but it never seems to work out. Mind if I have another?" he said over his shoulder as he headed toward the back of the store and the cooler.

Dick spoke after him as he watched him come back to the table and open the beer, "Gosh, you must have met a lot of people and seen a lot of stuff. Have you been to New York City?" Ben nodded. "Mexico?" Ben nodded.

"Gosh," said Dick.

This time as Ben's arm went up to bring the beer to his mouth, Dick noticed the jagged long scar running down the outer surface of Ben's right arm. The sort of scar that made you wince.

"Gosh, what happened to your arm?"

Ben rotated his arm in, transferring the beer to the other hand and looked at his arm. "Oh that. Football injury in college. I was a quarterback. Some son-of-a-bitch hit me so hard he broke my arm. I was already down on the ground. I had to have surgery."

Dick said, "Gosh, why did they cut it in such a weird way?"

Ben said, "I don't know. I guess they had to to get all the screws and metal plates in there."

Dick asked, "Does it hurt?"

Ben replied, "No, only when I watch football games," and broke into a broad grin, punctuated at the end by a long draw on the beer.

Dick looked at his beer. Ben was almost done with his second and he had barely drunk a third of his. (Ben will think I don't like to drink beer with him.) Dick took a long draw on his own bottle.

Sergeant Peterson looked up from his pad. "It was probably a knife wound or something like that. Guys like that get into fights, sometimes knife fights."

Dick responded, "Yeah, it could have been. God, I can't believe I felt sorry for the guy."

"What happened after that?" inquired the Sergeant.

Dick shook his head at his own memories, "Well, we sat around and talked and he drank a couple more beers. It started to get dark outside and I asked him if he wanted to stay for dinner. I cooked right there in the front of the store and we both had hamburgers and beans. He did most of the talking. He told me about lots of towns and places he had been and people he had met. He'd been an actor in Hollywood for a while, a stunt man. He'd also been an oil driller on rigs in Oklahoma for a while. He'd been a lumberjack in Seattle or somewhere near there. He also worked for the government for a while. Something in Washington or Virginia, although he wouldn't tell me the details. He told me it was too secret. He also said he had been to Vietnam, although he seemed awfully young for that. He must have been just a kid there. Maybe he lied about his age to get in. At any rate, he needed a place to stay. It turned out that somebody had broken into his hotel room the night before. I think he said it was the Radisson Hotel in Phoenix and had stolen all of his money while he was downstairs eating dinner. He didn't know what he was going to do. So, I put him up in the spare room and he stayed the night and the next thing I know I had offered him a job the next day. It felt so good to have somebody around. God, could he tell stories."

The Sergeant nodded, "So you gave him a job."

Dick replied, "Yeah."

"What did he do?"

"Well, he managed the pumps. Of course there isn't much business there, and he ran the store. We'd take turns. Things seemed to go all right for a couple of days and then I noticed most of the beer in the fridge was gone, but I didn't want to say anything to him. I thought maybe he drank because of the pain."

The Sergeant asked, "The pain?"

Dick replied, "Oh you know, the pain in his arm, and the wife, and the little girls and all, and losing that job in Chicago."

"At any rate, about a week later, two guys stopped to get some gas and buy some beer and chips and stuff. I'd never seen them before. They weren't from around here. Anyway, one of them called Ben 'Cowboy,' I suppose because of his boots. Ben got that big smile on his face, stared at the guy, and after he had finished filling up their tank pulled out the pump handle and sprayed gas on the side of their car. It could happen by accident, but he did it on purpose.

Anyway, this guy walked over to him and said, "You got a problem? You got a problem?" and Ben just kept on smiling. Then all of a sudden, so quick I didn't even see it, Ben had hit the guy in the head and knocked him down. When the guy tried to get up, Ben kicked him in the side. And he just kept right on smiling. The other guy dragged his friend into the car and they took off. I was afraid to say anything, but it scared me. Ben and I didn't talk anymore that night. I just went to bed. I had trouble getting to sleep. When I woke up in the morning he was gone."

The Sergeant asked, "Gone?"

Dick replied, "Yeah, gone and so was the money—gone—and so was my wife's sterling silver set—gone. All the drawers were open, the front door was open, and he was gone."

II

Ben Steele was cruising westward on his motorcycle, enjoying the wind, enjoying the open air, and starting to get thirsty. The beer buzz from lunch was wearing off, and it was past time to find a cool one someplace. Money was a problem. He had enough to keep him going for a week or so but that was only if he was real careful with what he ate and drank and where he slept. He needed to get some work or he needed to score. He'd do the former if he had to, but preferred the latter. He was too smart now to do anything to get caught. He knew how cops worked. He was never going to do time again. He found life inside hell and would never go back. Up ahead he spied an isolated gas station and house next to the highway. (This looks fine. Time for a beer.) He throttled the bike back and pulled in between the pumps and the door to the station. An old guy was standing in the doorway wearing a dirty, torn cowboy hat, a red plaid shirt that had seen better days, and a pair of scruffy cowboy boots.

(What a hayseed. I want a cold beer.)

"Howdy. Got anything cold to drink in there?" he said in a friendly way, flashing his million dollar smile, and starting to turn on the charm. (What a hayseed, but a meal ticket. Beer, groceries, a place to hang for a few days, and a travel bonus to boot.)

Less than a week later he had had it. It was kind of fun screwing with this hayseed's head but he was tired of it. He was tired of the old man's bad cooking, his stories about his dead wife, and he liked pumping gas about as well as he liked prison. Time to move on.

(God, people are gullible. You could tell them anything and they would believe it.) He smiled to himself and shook his head. That night after the hayseed went to bed, he had a couple more beers, emptied the cash register (the hayseed never locked it), and took the silver teapot, coffee server and tray, wrapped them in a towel and put them in a sack (must be worth something. I'll sell them when I get into town), and hit the road, looking for new horizons and new opportunities, and someplace to buy a beer in about two hours.

☐ Discussion

Ben clearly is unable to conform his behavior to acceptable social norms and engages in illegal acts (theft), repeatedly lies, appears to be impulsive (at least in the incident when he knocks down another individual), and is aggressive (as evidenced in the same altercation). We have no evidence that he feels remorse. The character portrayed is an adult. We don't know about his adjustment prior to age 18 but we can make certain assumptions based on his personality at this point.

Antisocial personality is more common in males than females, with an overall prevalence of around 2%. Symptoms of conduct disorder are present in these individuals by age 15. The course of the illness is chronic, although many of these individuals mellow by the fourth decade of life when there is a decrease in overall behavioral problems. There is strong evidence of familial increase in the risk of antisocial personality in male relatives of individuals with this disorder, and of somatization disorder in their female relatives. Males with antisocial personality are at high rate for substance-related disorders. Many of the features are also suggestive of other Axis II cluster B disorders including narcissistic, histrionic, and borderline personality disorder. This disorder is more common in those in lower socioeconomic groups, and in urban settings.

Treatments for antisocial personality disorder are not well developed. Many of these individuals end up dying prematurely in violent ways or in vehicular accidents, or eventually are incarcerated because of their illegal activities. Individuals with antisocial personality do not see themselves as having a disorder and are not usually interested in treatment.

☐ Questions for Further Discussion

1) Do you think it would be possible for individuals with this disorder to be outwardly successful (achieve a good income, good jobs, a family, etc.)?
2) How do you think individuals with this disorder would function when incarcerated?
3) Do you find Ben an attractive individual?

☐ References

American Psychiatric Association. (1994). *Diagnostic and statistical manual of mental disorders* (4th ed). Washington, DC: Author.

☐ Suggested Readings

Arnett, P. A. (1997). Autonomic responsivity in psychopaths: A critical review and theoretical proposal. *Clinical Psychology Review, 17,* 903–936.

Cunningham, M. D., & Reidy, T. J. (1998). Antisocial personality disorder an dpsychopathy: Diagnostic dilemmas in classifying patterns of antisocial behavior in sentencing evaluations. *Behavioral Science Law, 16,* 333–351.

Dinwiddie, S. H. (1996). Genetics, antisocial personality, and criminal responsibility. *Bulletin of the American Academy of Psychiatry Law, 24,* 95–108.

Eronen, M., Angermeyer, M. C., & Schulze, B. (1998). The psychiatric epidemiology of violent behavior. *Social Psychiatry and Psychiatric Epidemiology, 33,* S13–S23.

Geberth, V. J., & Turco, R. N. (1997). Antisocial personality disorder, sexual sadism, malignant narcissism, and serial murder. *Journal of Forensic Science, 42,* 49–60.

Hodgins, S. (1998). Epidemiological investigations of the associations between major mental disorders and crime: Methodological limitations and validity of the conclusions. *Social Psychiatry and Psychiatric Epidemiology, 33,* S29–S37.

Lilienfeld, S. O. (1998). Methodological advances and developments in the assessment of psychopathy. *Behavior and Research Therapy, 36,* 99–125.

Lynman, D. T. (1996). Early identification of chronic offenders: Who is the fledgling psychopath? *Psychological Bulletin, 120,* 209–234.

O'Connor, T. G., McGuire, S., Reiss, D., Hetherington, E. M., & Plomin, R. (1998). Co-occurrence of depression systems and antisocial behavior in adolescence: A common genetic liability. *Journal of Abnormal Psychology, 107,* 27–37.

Pajer, K. A. (1998). What happens to "bad" girls? A review of the adult outcomes of antisocial adolescent girls. *American Journal of Psychiatry, 155,* 862–870.

Paris, J. (1996). Antisocial personality disorder: A biopsychosocial model. *Canadian Journal of Psychiatry, 41,* 75–80.

Paris, J. (1997). Antiscial and borderline personality disorders: Two separate diagnoses or two aspects of the same psychopathology? *Comprehensive Psychiatry, 38,* 237–242.

Robertson, M. D., Bray, A., & Parker, G. B. (1996). Sociopathy: Forever forensic? *Medical Journal of Australia, 164,* 304–307.

Sanislow, C. A., & McGlashan, T. H. (1998). Treatment outcome of personality disorders. *Canadian Journal of Psychiatry, 43,* 237–250.

Shea, M. T., Widiger, T. A., & Klein, M. H. (1992). Comorbidity of personality disorders and depression: Implications for treatment. *Journal of Consulting Clinical Psychology, 60,* 857–868.

van den Bree, M. G., Svikis, D. S., & Pickens, R. W. (1998). Genetic influences in antisocial personality and drug use disorders. *Drug and Alcohol Dependence, 49,* 177–187.

Werry, J. S. (1997). Severe conduct disorder—some key issues. *Canadian Journal of Psychiatry, 42,* 577–583.

CONCLUSIONS

Readers who have negotiated the text to this point hopefully find themselves much better informed about the common forms of psychopathology. In creating these stories, although I have stressed the signs and symptoms of the individual syndromes, I have also attempted to make it abundantly clear that these are not stories about illnesses, but instead stories about people. Although their illnesses differ, at times dramatically, what the subjects of these stories have in common is their humanity. This is an important point, given that physicians and other healthcare providers sometimes refer to patients as if they were defined by their illness. A person may be referred to as a "schizophrenic" or an "anorectic" by a psychiatrist or, in other areas of medicine, a "diabetic" or an "epileptic." But people are not illnesses, and it is dehumanizing to think of them as such. This is particularly problematic for people who suffer from mental illnesses. It is easy at times, because their behavior may be difficult to understand or at times even seem bizarre, to forget that they are really people with illnesses, and that they need the same understanding and encouragement as everyone else. It has been all too easy to ignore the humanity of the mentally ill, particularly of the seriously mentally ill, who have often in the past been relegated to prison-like treatment facilities or, in the case of the Nazi, to gas chambers.

Are the mentally ill different from us? Not really, if we remember that the woman next door may suffer from depression, that the man behind the counter at the drugstore may have panic attacks, that the son of a friend may suffer from schizophrenia, and that you or I may at some time develop a mental illness. It's not "them," it's "us."

Our knowledge concerning mental illness, and the stigma associated with these illnesses are changing, but much stigma remains. However, it seems paradoxical, that as our knowledge of these conditions and the effectiveness of our treatments increase that the percentage of

213

Americans who have no health insurance or inadequate coverage for mental illnesses continues to grow. What good are treatments if people can't receive them? Many people with severe mental illness are already on the fringe of society, and many do not have access to the jobs that would provide them with the insurance they need. This situation seems to me inexcusable for a country that purports to provide equal rights to all its citizens.

Thus in closing, I encourage those students of psychopathology who read this work to learn the diagnostic schema well, to learn the subtle and the not-so-subtle differences among the various forms of mental illness, but most importantly, to not forget the humanity of the mentally ill, and to advocate for their acceptance and treatment.

James Mitchell, M.D.
Fargo, North Dakota
5/3/00

INDEX